CANADA

BY KURT WALDENDORF

Essential Library

An Imprint of Abdo Publishing

abdobooks.com

ABDOBOOKS.COM
Published by Abdo Publishing, a division of ABDO, PO Box 398166, Minneapolis, Minnesota 55439.

Printed in China.
052025
092025

Cover Photos: Sergii Figurnyi/Shutterstock Images (Niagara Falls); Darya Kozlovskikh/Shutterstock Images (pattern)
Interior Photos: Shutterstock Images, 4–5, 8, 9, 16 (globe), 18, 23, 24, 31, 35, 44, 60, 66, 79, 86–87, 89, 101; Eric L. Tollstam/Shutterstock Images, 6; Minas Panagiotakis/Getty Images Sport/Getty Images, 12; Russ Heinl/Shutterstock Images, 14–15, 20; Red Line Editorial, 16 (map); Jim Cumming/Shutterstock Images, 26–27; Sergey Uryadnikov/Shutterstock Images, 28; Christian Musat/Shutterstock Images, 32; Kens Canning/Shutterstock Images, 34; Feng Yu/Shutterstock Images, 37; Harry Beugelink/Shutterstock Images, 38–39; Eye Ubiquitous/Universal Images Group/Getty Images, 40; George Konig/Keystone Features/Hulton Archive/Getty Images, 42; Bildagentur-Online/Universal Images Group/Getty Images, 47; Hulton Archive/Getty Images, 49; Cole Burston/AFP/Getty Images, 50, 88; Jeff Whyte/Shutterstock Images, 52–53; Marc Bruxelle/Alamy, 56, 85; Leah Hennel/Getty Images Sport/Getty Images, 58; L. Paul Mann/Shutterstock Images, 61; Bruce Bennett Studios/Getty Images Studios/Getty Images, 62; Gilberto Mesquita/Shutterstock Images, 64–65; Dave Chan/AFP/Getty Images, 67; Sean Kilpatrick/AFP/Getty Images, 68; Sean Kilpatrick/The Canadian Press/AP Images, 71; Alexis Aubin/AFP/Getty Images, 72; Dima Zel/Shutterstock Images, 75; Marina Poushkina/Shutterstock Images, 76–77; FPG/Archive Photos/Getty Images, 78; Artem Onoprienko/Shutterstock Images, 82; Liang Sen/Xinhua News Agency/Getty Images, 90–91; Pierre Leclerc/Shutterstock Images, 94–95; BC Wildfire Service/The Canadian Press/AP Images, 97; Artur Widak/NurPhoto/Getty Images, 98

Editor: Marie Pearson
Series Designer: Maggie Villaume

Library of Congress Control Number: 2024948607

PUBLISHER'S CATALOGING-IN-PUBLICATION DATA
Names: Waldendorf, Kurt, author.
Title: Canada / by Kurt Waldendorf
Description: Minneapolis, Minnesota: Abdo Publishing, 2026 | Series: Essential library of countries | Includes online resources and index.
Identifiers: ISBN 9781098296957 (lib. bdg.) | ISBN 9798384919476 (ebook)
Subjects: LCSH: Geography--Juvenile literature. | Canada--Juvenile literature. | North America--Juvenile literature. | Canada--History--Juvenile literature.
Classification: DDC 971--dc23

CONTENTS

CHAPTER **ONE**

A TOUR OF CANADA

As the plane descends, Jayda's eyes pop open. She checks the time. The early morning flight from Detroit, Michigan, has been in the air less than two hours. But through the plane window, Jayda can already see her destination, a sprawling city beside a wide river.

Months ago, Jayda's mom learned she'd be traveling to Montreal, Canada, on business. Jayda's parents had decided to make it a family trip and spend the weekend exploring the city together. They were traveling only a few hundred miles, but the trip had been months in the making. Jayda and her little brother, John, had to get passports before they could visit the United States' northern neighbor.

Mount Royal in Montreal, Canada, turns beautiful colors in autumn. Mount Royal Park was established in 1876.

Some shops and restaurants in Old Montreal are inside historic buildings. Visitors can learn about history while they shop.

As the plane gets closer, Jayda bounces in her seat. Through the window, she can already pick out some of the places she's read about. There's the massive Champlain Bridge, which spans the Saint Lawrence River; the leaning Montreal Tower, built for the 1976 Summer Olympic Games; and Mount Royal, the hilly park in the middle of Montreal, already showing its fall colors. Jayda is looking forward to everything her family has planned. There will be a blend of old and new with historical sites and modern locations. But she's most excited to watch her favorite hockey team, the Detroit Red Wings, take on the Montreal Canadiens that night.

After the plane lands, Jayda and her family make their way to security. Along the way, Jayda sees that the signs are in both English and French. A border agent checks each family member's passport. After asking Jayda a few questions, the agent smiles. "*Bienvenue à Montréal*," she says, which is French for "Welcome to Montreal."

Montreal is the largest city in the Canadian province of Quebec. Unlike the other provinces and territories, where English is the primary language, Quebec's official language is French. "*Merci beaucoup*—thank you very much," Jayda says as she moves past the guard.

MOUNT ROYAL

At 820 feet (250 m) tall, Mount Royal is a short mountain with big significance.[1] The site was visited by the first French explorer to the region, Jacques Cartier, who gave it its current name in 1535. Culturally, it has been an important site for leisure. In 1874, the city hired Frederick Law Olmsted to design a park for the mountain. Olmsted had designed New York City's Central Park. Today, the hilly Mount Royal park provides a getaway in the large city. Every Sunday in the summer, people gather on the mountain to play music and socialize.

OLD MONTREAL

Jayda and her family are staying in Old Montreal. This is the historic center of the city. After dropping off their luggage at the hotel, they go to join a walking tour of Montreal.

The buildings in this part of the city look very old. The cobblestone streets remind Jayda of the historic parts of Detroit. The air has a similar fall chill. But Old Montreal is different too. The streets are filled with pedestrians. Rows of colorful shops and restaurants line the streets. Some have outdoor seating, where people are eating bagels and sipping lattes. Jayda hears more French being spoken than she did at the airport, and nearly all the signs are in French. She wonders how there came to be such a strong French influence on the city.

At the tour's first stop, Jayda gets some answers. Jacques Cartier Square is a large plaza in the heart of Old Montreal. It's named for the French explorer who first visited the site in 1535. Cartier went on to claim the region for France, a move that brought thousands of French traders and settlers to the area in the 1600s. Eventually, the British took control of the country. But the people of Quebec, known as Quebecois, remain proud of the province's French heritage.

As the tour continues, Jayda learns more about the city's French roots. Her favorite stop is the Notre-Dame Basilica. The outside of the building reminds her of pictures she's seen

"LONG LIVE FREE QUEBEC"

Because of the strong French influence in Quebec, some citizens have pushed for the province to separate from the rest of Canada. In 1967, French president Charles de Gaulle gave a memorable speech from a balcony overlooking Jacques Cartier Square. He ended the speech saying, "*Vive le Québec libre*," which means "Long live free Quebec." The speech caused an international controversy. Many people, including world leaders, thought he was pushing for Quebec to separate from Canada. The phrase continues to be a rallying cry for people who support Quebec independence.

of the Notre-Dame cathedral in Paris, France. Two bell towers rise to more than 215 feet (66 m).[2] Between them is a grand entrance of high-arching doorways.

The inside is even more impressive. The colorful sanctuary is filled with intricate carvings and expertly crafted stained glass. Jayda learns that the site of the church dates to the earliest days of the French settlement. She can hardly believe she's walking the same ground as some of the first European explorers on the continent.

Notre-Dame's chapel was destroyed by a fire in 1978. The modern chapel was completed in 1982.

MONTREAL TODAY

After the tour, Jayda and her family get a taste of newer additions to Montreal's cultural heritage. For much of Canada's history, the nation has been a popular destination for immigrants. In Montreal, many Chinese, Italian, Portuguese, and West Indian people put down roots, and the city continues to welcome many immigrants today.

Montreal is a popular tourist destination, attracting 11 million visitors each year.[4]

For lunch, Jayda's family heads to a popular Mediterranean restaurant overlooking the Saint Lawrence River. As Jayda digs into a seafood dish, John points excitedly to a ship slowly making its way along the river. The ship is so big, he says he thinks it must have taken a wrong turn. Jayda knows the ship is called a laker, and it's just getting started on a long trip through the Great Lakes. She wonders what its massive hull might contain.

After lunch, the family walks to nearby Chinatown to try Montreal's famous dragon's beard candy. Jayda watches as a man stretches a thick, sugary substance into hundreds of thin, hairlike strands before adding peanuts, coconut, sesame seeds, and chocolate. The sweet treat is not like anything Jada has tried before.

Next, the family heads underground to take the metro, or subway, to the Montreal Museum of Fine Arts. The largest art museum in Canada, it contains more than 41,000 works from around the world, including famous historical and contemporary pieces.[3] Jayda and her family spend most of their time exploring the Quebec and Canadian art collection.

A room of landscape paintings catches Jayda's eye. Each one depicts a different Canadian landscape. One shows a colorful fishing village on the coast of the province of Nova Scotia. Another shows the northern lights.

After a few minutes, John pulls Jayda forward to the next room. The space is filled with art from Indigenous communities in Canada. He leads her to a display of Inuit carvings. Jayda learns

> **UNDERGROUND CITY**
>
> Like many Canadian cities, Montreal endures frigid conditions in the winter. Montreal's Underground City allows residents and visitors to keep warm. What began as a series of underground subway stations now consists of more than 21 miles (33 km) of pedestrian tunnels.[5] But the Underground City is more than just a way to get around. With many shops and restaurants as well as a number of hotels and movie theaters, it is also a destination. In theory, a person could live a full life in Montreal without going outside.

that each one is made from a black material called soapstone, which the Inuit have used for more than 7,000 years. John's favorite shows a curious-looking walrus with long tusks. Jayda favors one shaped like a snowy owl.

As Jayda continues through the exhibit, she feels as if she could spend hours admiring the artwork and learning about its meaning. She wishes she could visit the other collections at the museum, which range from Inuit art and international pieces to contemporary art and an outdoor sculpture garden. But before long, her mom reminds her of the time. They don't want to be late for the game.

A NATIONAL PASTIME

After stopping back at the hotel to put on her Red Wings jersey, Jayda and her family head to Bell Centre. The building is home to the oldest professional ice hockey team in the world, the Montreal Canadiens. The team is one of seven Canadian squads in the National Hockey League (NHL).

The United States has more teams in the NHL than Canada does. However, many of the sport's top players come from Canada, and hockey ranks as the most popular sport in the country.

Cole Caufield joined the Montreal Canadiens in 2021. He signed an eight-year contract with the team in 2023.

Jayda feels this enthusiasm as she and her family wade through a sea of red Canadiens jerseys in the halls of the arena. Once seated, Jayda notices banners commemorating the Canadiens' 24 Stanley Cup titles, the most of any NHL team.[6] Large jerseys hang from the rafters, paying tribute to team legends.

Just before game time, the players line up at center ice for the country's national anthem. The lights dim, and the more than 21,000 fans stand and hold their hands over their hearts.[7] A Canadian flag appears on the ice, and the music for "O Canada" begins.

Goosebumps spread along Jayda's arms as the crowd sings along with the anthem, first in French and then in English. Jayda has been to many hockey games, but this experience is unlike any she's had before. Even though she's been in the country only a short time, she feels she's gotten a glimpse of Canadian culture and why Canadians are proud of their country. As the puck drops, Jayda still plans to cheer for her hometown team, but she also hopes her parents will plan another visit to Canada soon.

BEYOND MONTREAL

Canada is a vast and varied land. Its provinces and territories stretch across six different time zones and span more than half of the Northern Hemisphere.[8] Canada is filled with natural beauty. From the rocky Nova Scotia shores to the lakes and prairies of Manitoba to the coastal rainforests of British Columbia, the country offers an array of landscapes to explore.

Likewise, Canadian cities feature diverse cultural experiences. Distinct French, English, and Indigenous influences have been present since the country's early days. And over the years, immigrants from around the world have added new components to the cultural mix. While Canada's history is one that includes discrimination, conflict, and war, Canadians take pride in the rich tapestry of cultures that has developed today.

CHAPTER **TWO**

GEOGRAPHY

Canada makes up a large portion of the North American continent. Covering an area of 3,855,103 square miles (9,984,671 sq km), it has the second-largest area of any country in the world, behind Russia. To Canada's south, it shares a border with 12 US states, and to the northwest, it borders the state of Alaska. The US–Canada border stretches 5,524 miles (8,890 km), making it the longest land border between two countries.[1]

Canada also borders water on three sides. The Atlantic Ocean sits to the east. The Pacific Ocean lies to the west. To the north, Canada's Arctic Archipelago, which is made of more than 36,000 islands, stretches far into the Arctic Ocean.[2] Due in large part to the Arctic Archipelago, Canada has the longest coastline of any nation in the world, measuring about

Canada has a varied landscape, which includes more than 52,000 islands.

MAP OF CANADA

KEY:

- Capital
- City
- Point of Interest

Ellesmere Island
ARCTIC OCEAN
GREENLAND
BAFFIN BAY
Yukon River
Mackenzie River
Great Bear Lake
Great Slave Lake
N
W
E
S
Haida Gwaii
PACIFIC OCEAN
HUDSON BAY
Jasper National Park
Edmonton
Vancouver
Saskatchewan River
Victoria
Calgary
Gros Morne National Park
NEWFOUNDLAND
Lake Winnipeg
Winnipeg
Le Massif de Charlevoix
Lake Superior
Quebec
Ottawa
Montreal
Toronto
Lake Ontario
UNITED STATES OF AMERICA
ATLANTIC OCEAN

126,000 miles (203,000 km).[3] To the northeast, Canada shares a sea border with Greenland, which is also the longest border of its kind between two nations.

LAY OF THE LAND

Politically, Canada is divided into ten provinces and three territories. The provinces are similar to US states. Each has its own capital city, constitution, and government. Canada's provinces are Prince Edward Island, Nova Scotia, New Brunswick, Newfoundland and Labrador, Ontario, Quebec, Manitoba, Saskatchewan, Alberta, and British Columbia.

Canada's territories are similar in structure, but due in part to their low populations, they do not have provincial governments and fall under federal control. The territories are Nunavut, Yukon, and the Northwest Territories. Together, the three are often called the Northern Territories.

Canada's provinces and territories are spread across multiple geographic regions, including the Canadian Shield, the Interior Plains, the Great Lakes–Saint Lawrence Lowlands, the Appalachian Region, the Western Cordillera, and the Arctic Archipelago. One way to think about these regions is to imagine Canada as a large basin with mountain ranges on three sides and flatter, lower-lying land in the middle.

The Canadian Shield is the largest portion of the low-lying interior of the country. Forming a shield-like curve around Hudson Bay, it includes parts of eight provinces and territories and makes up nearly 50 percent of Canada's land area.[4] The Canadian Shield is part of the oldest and most geologically stable section of the North American continent.

While other regions have been shaped by the movement of shifting slabs of Earth's crust called tectonic plates, the Canadian Shield has remained in place. The rocks in this region are very old, with some dating back more than four billion years. They became exposed during the last ice age, when glaciers scraped clear the region's surface. Today, the hilly, rocky surface remains exposed, making it an important region for Canada's mining industry and a difficult place for people to live.

To the west of the Canadian Shield are the Interior Plains. As glaciers moved through this region, they left behind stone, gravel, sand, and dirt. As a result, the Interior Plains have higher elevations, flatter lands, and richer soils than the Canadian Shield. Farming and ranching are common in the southern portion of the plains.

In the northern plains, forestry, mining, and fossil fuel extraction are important industries. Like the Midwestern United States, the Interior Plains are sparsely populated. However, a few large cities dot the landscape, including Winnipeg in Manitoba, Regina in Saskatchewan, and Calgary and Edmonton in Alberta.

ERRATICS AND ESKERS

Evidence of ancient glacial activity is found across the Canadian Shield in the form of erratics and eskers. Erratics are chunks of rock that glaciers scraped away and transported elsewhere. They range from the size of a pebble to boulders more than 100 feet (30 m) wide and can be carried more than 1,000 miles (1,610 km).[5] Eskers are created by rivers flowing through glaciers. These rivers carry sediment that builds up over time. Today, this sediment takes the form of long, curving mounds of earth that stretch across the surface of the Canadian Shield.

The Great Lakes–Saint Lawrence Lowlands make up a small but important portion of Canada's interior. Here, the glaciers that moved across the Canadian Shield and Interior Plains melted, leaving a region filled with fresh water. Located in southern Quebec and Ontario, these lowlands make up only 2 percent of Canada's land area.[6] But due to the region's milder climate, rich soil, and closeness to the United States, it is one of Canada's top agricultural, industrial, and cultural areas.

The Great Lakes–Saint Lawrence Lowlands include major cities such as Ottawa and Toronto in Ontario and Montreal and Quebec City in Quebec. In total, the region is home to more than 50 percent of Canada's population. It has almost 25 percent of Canada's agricultural production.[7]

GLACIERS TODAY

Canada is home to more than 77,220 square miles (200,000 sq km) of glaciers, an area larger than the US state of Nebraska. Some are alpine glaciers found high in mountains. Others are continental glaciers, which form in areas that are very cold year-round. Every glacier goes through a continual process of melting along the edges while reforming in the center. But during the past 200 years, warmer temperatures have caused Canadian glaciers to melt faster than they can reform. Scientists predict that from 2005 to 2100, glaciers in Alberta and British Columbia will lose 70 percent of their volume.[8]

To the east of the lowlands is the Appalachian Region. Here the Appalachian Mountains extend north from the United States into Nova Scotia, New Brunswick, and Newfoundland and Labrador, forming the eastern rim of the continental basin. The Appalachians are the oldest mountain range on the continent, dating back about 480 million years. The range's peaks have been worn down by erosion, making the region more inhabited

Thousand Islands National Park on the Saint Lawrence River contains more than 1,800 islands.

than other Canadian mountain ranges. But stunning natural sights are still present. Gros Morne National Park in Newfoundland is known for its dramatic fjords and coastal peaks. It is a United Nations Educational, Scientific and Cultural Organization (UNESCO) World Heritage site.

The western rim of the continental basin is formed by the Rocky Mountains, which extend north from the United States through British Columbia and into the Yukon and Northwest Territories. Together with the Columbia Mountains, Cariboo Mountains, and Coast Mountains, the Canadian Rockies form the Western Cordillera region. The young peaks of the Western Cordillera formed around 80 million years ago, when large tectonic plates collided. The range is home to North America's second-tallest peak, Mount Logan, which rises to 19,551 feet (5,959 m).[9]

Much of the Western Cordillera is sparsely populated due to its rugged terrain. However, cities along the coast of British Columbia such as Victoria and Vancouver are heavily populated. These cities make this region one of the more populous regions in Canada.

The Arctic Archipelago is the northernmost Canadian region. The archipelago begins as low-lying tundra in the south and ascends into the Innuitian Mountains. These mountains form the northern rim of the continental basin.

The Arctic Archipelago is the coldest, driest, and least-populated region in Canada. It includes the historic homeland of the Inuit, and many Inuit still live in the region. The region is also home to military personnel who patrol Canada's northern border. A military base known as Alert, located on Ellesmere Island, is the northernmost permanently inhabited place in the world. The permanent residents work for the Canadian armed forces and government.

FRESH WATER AND COASTS

In addition to its striking geological formations, Canada's landscape is distinguished by plentiful water resources. Despite having less than 0.5 percent of the global population, Canada claims 20 percent of the world's fresh water.[10] These resources come in many forms.

The Great Lakes region is home to the world's second- and fourth-largest lakes, Lake Superior and Lake Huron, which are shared with the United States. Additionally, the border between the Canadian Shield and the Interior Plains holds Great Bear Lake, Great Slave Lake, and Lake Winnipeg. These are the eighth-, tenth-, and twelfth-largest lakes in the world, respectively.[11]

Canada also has several important rivers. They include the Mackenzie, which flows into the Arctic Ocean; the Saint Lawrence, which flows into the Atlantic Ocean; and the Yukon, which travels to the Pacific Ocean. Each of these rivers, along with the freshwater lakes they connect, remain invaluable in supporting Canada's people, ecosystems, and economy.

Canada's fresh water also contributes to some of its most stunning attractions. The snow-filled peaks of the Western Cordillera provide world-class skiing

A FABLED RIVER

In 1789, Scottish explorer Alexander Mackenzie set out in search of a water route connecting the Atlantic and Pacific Oceans. He thought the river known locally as Dehcho would be part of this passage, connecting Lake Athabasca in northern Alberta to the Pacific Ocean. But when his canoe reached the end of the river, he was greeted by the whales of the Arctic Ocean instead. It wasn't the passage Mackenzie had hoped for, but he'd become the first European to travel Canada's longest river, which was later named after him.

Ellesmere Island is home to mountains and glaciers. It covers 75,767 square miles (196,236 sq km).

About 65 percent of Canada is covered in snow for at least six months of the year.

and snowboarding opportunities. The Athabasca Glacier in Jasper National Park is a UNESCO World Heritage site and one of the most accessible glaciers in the world. Niagara Falls between Lake Erie and Lake Ontario attracts more than 12 million visitors each year.[12]

But while fresh water is plentiful in Canada, it is not present everywhere. Less than half of Canada's fresh water comes from renewable sources such as lakes and rivers.[13] The rest is found in sources such as glaciers and underground aquifers. Most of Canada's rivers flow north, leaving some areas in the south without easy freshwater access.

CLIMATE

Canada is known for winter activities such as hockey and for Arctic animals such as polar bears. This cold-weather reputation is well earned. Most of Canada has a winter season in which the average temperature is below freezing. But during the rest of the year, conditions vary dramatically.

Ocean air currents play an important role in determining the climate of each location. On the western coast, winds blowing from the Pacific Ocean bring heavy rain. Some areas in British Columbia receive more than 100 inches (250 cm) of precipitation annually, creating rainforest conditions.[14] Ocean winds also keep coastal temperatures more moderate. As a result, cities such as Victoria and Vancouver are among the few Canadian cities with average winter temperatures above freezing. Air currents blowing west across the Great Lakes and north along the Atlantic Coast have similar effects, bringing 30 to 50 inches (76–127 cm) of rainfall and more moderate temperatures to these regions.[15]

At more than 2,000 feet (610 m) deep, Great Slave Lake is North America's deepest lake and one of the deepest on Earth.[18]

Canada's interior experiences more significant extremes. The coldest Canadian temperature, −81 degrees Fahrenheit (−63°C), occurred inland at Snag, Yukon. The warmest temperature, 113 degrees Fahrenheit (45°C), was recorded inland at Midale, Saskatchewan.[16] The northern Interior Plains and Arctic Archipelago receive little rainfall, creating polar deserts. Due in part to the extreme conditions in these regions, more than two-thirds of Canadians live within 62 miles (100 km) of the southern border, and many large cities are concentrated around the Great Lakes.[17]

CHAPTER **THREE**

PLANTS AND ANIMALS

Canada is a country brimming with natural life. More than 8.5 percent of its land is covered in forest, making it the third-most-forested land in the world behind Brazil and Russia.[1] It also holds about a quarter of the world's wetlands and temperate rainforests.[2]

These massive, diverse landscapes feature a wide variety of species. They include the well-known beaver and moose, along with thousands of yet-to-be-identified species of insects, fish, and fungi. In all, an estimated 80,000 species of plants and animals live in the country.[3]

The Canadian government has committed to protecting 30 percent of the country's land and water

The snowy owl breeds in the Canadian tundra. There are estimated to be more than 50,000 snowy owls in Canada.

Canada is home to about 16,000 polar bears. They hunt for seals on the sea ice.

habitats, an area four times larger than the state of Texas.[4] However, threats such as climate change and habitat loss remain. More than 600 plant and animal species are considered at risk and are under federal protection.[5]

FROZEN TUNDRA

Stretching across northern Canada, tundra covers about 40 percent of the country's surface.[6] The word *tundra* means "barren land," and the biome features harsh conditions. The ground is in a state of permafrost, which means it is always or nearly always frozen. High winds whip across the treeless landscape. Winters are long and dark. Arctic regions experience polar night, in which the sun remains below the horizon for long stretches. Summers are short and bright, with periods of near-constant sunlight.

Canada's tundra has difficult conditions. Yet it is home to nearly 2,000 plant species.[7] And throughout the year, at least 75 mammal species, 240 bird species, and 3,300 species of insects call this region home.[8]

Species that live in the tundra year-round are uniquely adapted to handle its challenges. Plants sprout in low-growing bunches to better shield themselves from wind and cold. Most are perennials, which means they spend a long time—sometimes years—gathering nutrients before blooming and spreading seeds.

With a flowering season as short as six weeks, tundra plants don't have much time to reproduce. Flowers begin blooming when there is still snow on the ground. Plants such as the

Arctic dryad turn slowly throughout the day, taking in as much sunlight as possible to spur the reproductive process. Other plants reproduce on their own. The Arctic poppy pushes out underground growths called runners, which eventually become new plants.

Up to three billion birds migrate north to breed in the boreal forest.[10]

Lichens exist in the tundra year-round. They can grow on rocks and survive with little moisture. Lichen consists of multiple organisms, such as fungi and algae, working together. The fungi form the organism's structure, and the algae provide energy through photosynthesis.

Plant-eating tundra animals include musk oxen, Arctic hares, lemmings, and caribou. These animals are preyed upon by Arctic foxes, Arctic wolves, and snowy owls. Along the coastline, polar bears prey on seals. Because of the extreme cold and long winters, hibernation is not an option for most tundra animals. To stay warm, mammals have developed specialized coats. Caribou have hollow hairs that trap heat near their bodies. Musk oxen grow a woolly layer of fur, which they shed each spring.

FOREST LIFE

South of the tundra, the landscape transitions into the boreal region. This forested region stretches from the Yukon–Alaska border in the west to Newfoundland and Labrador in the east. The region makes up 55 percent of the country's land area.[9]

Plants in the tundra can turn many beautiful colors in autumn.

The boreal region is dominated by evergreen forests. Species such as spruce, balsam fir, jack pine, and tamarack thrive. Snow slips easily from the branches of these cone-shaped trees, keeping the wood from breaking. Waxy needles make the trees resistant to extremes such as drought and frost. The trees are also adapted to deal with wildfires, which are natural occurrences in this region. The black spruce has waxy cones that open with heat, allowing seeds to spread into burned areas. Poplar seeds spread on parachutes of fluff.

The boreal forest is home to some of Canada's most well-known mammals. Moose, deer, elk, black bears, brown bears, gray wolves, lynx, beavers, muskrats, martens, and mink all call this region home. So do birds such as jays, owls, and woodpeckers.

Snow accumulation is common in the boreal forest. Animals such as the lynx, snowshoe hare, and ptarmigan have developed snowshoe-like feet to stay atop the crust. Moose have long, skinny legs that help keep their bodies above snow level. Species such as black bears and wood frogs wait out winter's cold through hibernation.

The boreal forest is also a seasonal destination. In the north, herds of caribou overwinter in the forest before heading to the tundra to breed. Birds migrate north to the boreal forest in the spring to breed. About half of all bird species in the United States and Canada use the boreal forest.[11]

On the western coast, abundant rainfall and long growing seasons allow rainforests to grow. A thick canopy of coniferous trees such as Douglas fir, western hemlock, and western red cedar grows here. Some trees are more than 1,000 years old.[12] They can reach more than 300 feet (91 m) tall.[13]

Cooler temperatures make downed trees break down more slowly. As a result, trees decomposing on the forest floor become nurse logs. On these elevated surfaces, seeds sprout into seedlings, free from the

NATIONAL ANIMAL

The beaver became an official symbol of Canada in 1975, but its historical significance goes back much further. Before European colonization, the beaver was an important food source for Indigenous people. When Europeans arrived, the popularity of the beaver's waterproof fur spurred the exploration and eventual colonization of the area. This came at a great expense to beavers. When the fur trade began, millions of beavers lived in Canada. By the mid-1800s, the beaver was nearly extinct. Today, government protection has helped beaver populations recover.

competition of ferns and shrubs on the ground. Seedlings start growing before the logs fully break down. Epiphytes such as mosses and ferns have adapted to grow on top of other plants to reach light.

Black-tailed deer, gray wolves, grizzly bears, and black bears all call the temperate rainforest home. The Great Bear Rainforest is a protected area on the coast of British Columbia. It is home to the spirit bear, a rare type of black bear with ghostly white or cream-colored fur. Five species of salmon also travel through the temperate rainforest, offering an important food source for bears and coastal wolves.[14]

MAPLE PRIDE

Common in the southeastern forests, the sugar maple has long held special significance for people in Canada. Before colonization, Indigenous peoples used the tree's sap for medicinal purposes and to preserve meats. When French settlers arrived, going to the *cabane à sucre*, or sugar shack, to prepare maple syrup became an important cultural practice. During World War I (1914–1918), the maple leaf appeared on Canadian soldiers' helmets. In 1965, the maple leaf was chosen to appear on Canada's national flag, cementing its status as an iconic Canadian symbol.

LIFE ON THE PRAIRIE

The southern parts of Alberta, Saskatchewan, and Manitoba are home to prairie land. The native plants include varieties of shortgrass, sagebrush, and cacti. These plants have adapted to handle cold winters, hot summers, and long periods of drought. Sagebrush finds water by extending roots deep underground. Bluebunch wheatgrass uses its long, curved stalks to redirect rainwater toward the plant's roots. Flowers such as yellow bells sprout

British Columbia has more than half of Canada's grizzly bear population.

early in spring, completing their life cycle before the hottest and driest weather arrives.

The prairie is home to large plant eaters such as bison, mule deer, and elk. Smaller herbivores include prairie dogs, pocket gophers, and mice, which burrow underground for protection and to avoid winter's coldest months. Predators include badgers, coyotes, hawks, owls, and snakes.

Native Canadian prairies have been greatly changed by human influence. In the 1800s, settlers reduced the bison population in the region to near extinction, and few remain today. As the country developed economically, prairie land became popular for agriculture and ranching. Today, native prairie grasses have been replaced by crops such as wheat and canola.

Wetlands in southern Canada have also been affected. About 70 percent of the original wetlands in this region have been lost.[15] Prairie potholes, which are small depressions left

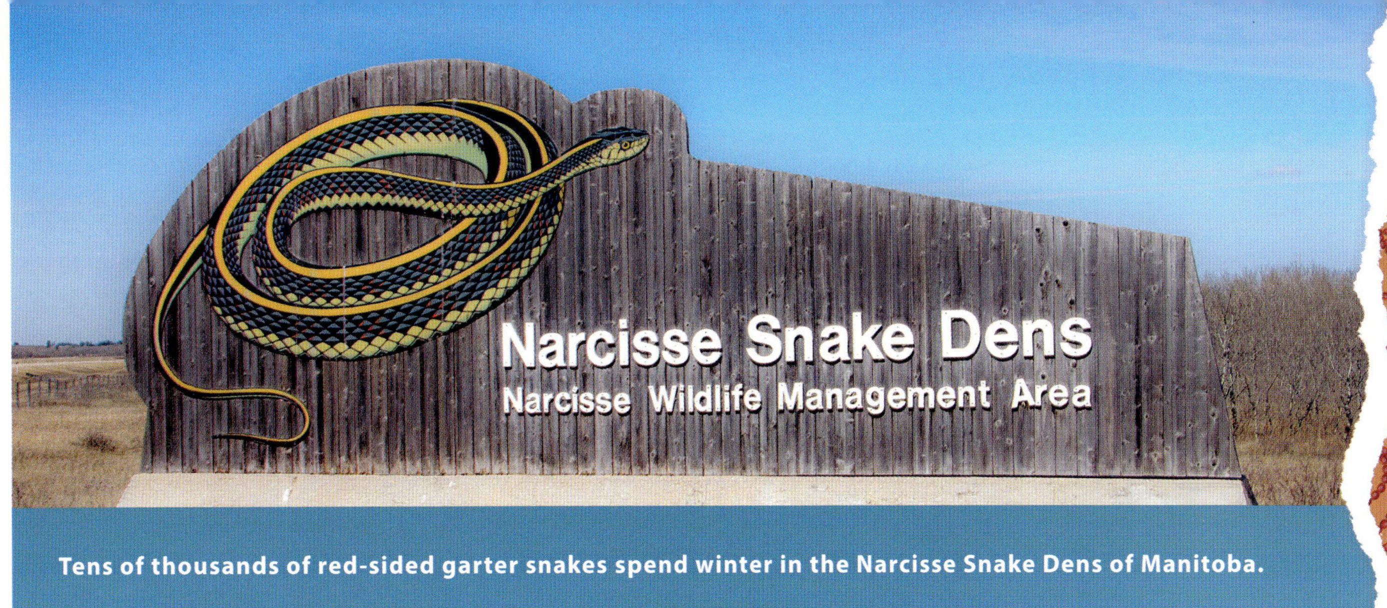

Tens of thousands of red-sided garter snakes spend winter in the Narcisse Snake Dens of Manitoba.

behind by glaciers, were filled in. Historically, these potholes helped waterfowl such as ducks and geese as they migrated through the region. As a result of these changes, the waterfowl population has dropped significantly from its historical numbers.

MARINE LIFE

Canada's coastal waters are also home to a rich variety of life, with each species particularly adapted to its environment. Along the Atlantic Coast, puffins are common. These seabirds have short, stiff wings that allow them to move underwater and find prey in the Atlantic's shallows. Their large, serrated beaks allow them to store up to 60 fish on a dive.[16]

Canada's Arctic waters are home to the beluga whale. The whale's distinct white color helps it blend in with the sea ice and avoid predators. On the Pacific coast, the sea otter uses a number of adaptations to survive the frigid temperatures. It has waterproof fur and can open and close its nose and ears to keep out cold water. By lying on its back and moving its feet in and out of the water, it can effectively regulate its body temperature.

THREATS AND CONSERVATION

Because Canadian plants and animals are adapted to survive in particular environments, small changes can have big impacts. Climate change poses a threat to many Canadian species. Melting sea ice in Canada's Arctic makes it more difficult for polar bears to hunt and for beluga whales to find shelter.

Changing conditions inland are affecting the caribou's migration patterns, at times keeping them from accessing food. Warming temperatures have increased the presence of pests and disease among some species. Moose have been significantly affected because winter tick populations have increased. The ticks force moose to spend more time grooming and less time searching for food.

Habitat loss also threatens Canadian species. Today, Canada has roughly 25 percent of its native grasslands remaining.[17] These lands are broken up by roads and developments. Animals such as the

MIGRATING MONARCHS

Canadian prairies have historically provided a habitat for an impressive migration. Each spring, monarch butterflies migrate north from Mexico. The lengthy journey to the northern United States and southern Canada spans three or four generations of butterflies. After spending the summer in the north, the monarchs reproduce once more and begin the migration back south. While monarchs still spend summers in Canada's southern prairies, loss of their natural habitat has forced much of the population to head east to the Great Lakes region.

burrowing owl and American badger, which rely on open areas with low vegetation to find prey, have been significantly affected. Logging activities have put animals such as the eastern cougar and Vancouver Island marmot at risk.

Since 2000, Canada has taken major steps to protect its natural habitats. It doubled the area of protected land and significantly increased the marine areas that are protected. The country is also home to several UNESCO Biosphere Reserves, which are identified as important sites for biological diversity. In addition to being protected, these reserves are places for research on human effects on the environment.

In 2002, Canada passed the Species at Risk Act to help prevent wildlife species from disappearing. Every five years, a committee releases a report assessing Canada's native species. It provides recovery plans for threatened or endangered species.

Burrowing owls make their nests in burrows other animals have dug.

CHAPTER **FOUR**

HISTORY

Humans first arrived on the North American continent more than 12,000 years ago, coming across a land bridge from Asia. At the time, the area now known as Canada was covered by glaciers, so people headed south into what are now the United States and Mexico. By about 10,000 years ago, the glaciers had retreated, and people had spread across nearly all of modern-day Canada.

Twelve major language groups developed across what is now Canada.[1] Across each language group, distinct political and cultural divisions developed. These varied greatly across the continent. In the Great Lakes region, agriculture was introduced around 1,500 years ago. The Wendat (Huron) and Haudenosaunee (Iroquois) used farming to supplement their hunting and gathering. They built permanent villages, some

Haida and other western coast First Nations people continue to influence the area. Haida artists carve totem poles, which stand in public spaces in Vancouver and elsewhere.

Blackfoot members continue to celebrate their traditions today. Some participate in traditional dances, such as the Jingle Dance.

with as many as 2,000 people.[2] An extensive trade network developed between tribes.

On the western coast, peoples such as the Haida found a consistent food source in salmon. The Haida built permanent settlements and became skilled craftspeople. They created large post-and-beam structures, dugout canoes, and artistic carvings.

Elsewhere, tribes were more isolated. On the southern plains, the Blackfoot relied on a nomadic way of life, hunting bison and collecting nuts and berries. In the northern plains, the Cree and Dene lived in small forest communities and hunted animals such as caribou, moose, and hare. Farther north, the Inuit hunted Arctic wildlife.

By the 1500s, an estimated 200,000 Indigenous people lived in what is now Canada.[3] Virtually all peoples were self-governing and politically independent. European settlers changed the ways of life for Indigenous people.

In the short term, many Indigenous people died from foreign diseases brought by settlers. In the long term, Indigenous peoples dealt with foreign powers who did not recognize their sovereignty and sought to change or erase their ways of life.

NEW ARRIVALS

In 1497, explorer John Cabot reached North America. The site he visited was said to be "New Found Launde" for England and would later become known as Newfoundland. Explorers ventured farther inland in 1534. During multiple expeditions, Jacques Cartier of France explored the Saint Lawrence River. During these trips, Cartier interacted with the Iroquois. He heard the word *kanata*, which means "village," and soon the word *Canada* was used to describe the land.

The 1600s brought waves of settlers to the continent. Motivated by demand for furs in Europe, the French king gave explorer Pierre du Gua a monopoly, or exclusive control, on trade in the region. Du Gua established the first settlement in an area that became known as New France. A few years later, Quebec City was established. The British built their first settlement in 1610 on the Atlantic Coast. Soon after, the Scots claimed Nova Scotia, which is Latin for "New Scotland."

In 1670, King Charles II of England granted the Hudson's Bay Company exclusive trading rights over the Hudson Bay watershed. For the next 100 years, the company competed with New France–based traders. Tensions rose. The French and English each allied with different Indigenous nations. A series of conflicts known as the French and Indian War (1754–1763) broke out. Eventually, the British defeated the French at Quebec City, ending France's North American empire.

Hudson's Bay Company was still processing beaver furs in Canada in the mid-1940s.

BRITISH RULE

Under British rule, New France became known as the Province of Quebec. Still, French culture remained strong. In an effort to better govern the region, the British Parliament passed the Quebec Act in 1774. The law allowed the French to practice Catholic Christianity rather than convert to England's Protestant Christianity. A Protestant is a member of one of the Christian denominations that separated from the Roman Catholic Church. The law also allowed French people to hold public office and preserved certain French laws.

The following year, war broke out to the south of the Province of Quebec. The United States had declared independence from Britain. The American Revolutionary War (1775–1783) began. Canadians were split about the war. Many British Canadians remained strong supporters of British authorities. But many French Canadians who were unhappy with British rule sympathized with the Americans.

To stave off conflict with disgruntled colonists in Canada, the British Parliament passed the Constitutional Act in 1791. It separated the Province of Quebec into Upper Canada and Lower Canada and gave each its own colonial government. The governments of Upper Canada and Lower Canada were set up to better address the concerns of British Canadians and French Canadians, respectively. Still, neither province was allowed to completely govern itself. The British government still directed policy decisions.

THE WAR OF 1812

Following the American Revolutionary War, conflict again broke out in the region in 1812. The US government was upset about British trade interference on the seas. The US Navy could not stand up to the British fleet, so instead, the Americans attempted to take Canada from the United Kingdom. In June, the United States launched an invasion, sparking the War of 1812 (1812 –1815). The British, along with Indigenous allies, repelled the attack, and the war ended without a clear winner.

DESIRING CHANGE

In the early 1800s, discontent with British rule grew in Upper and Lower Canada. From 1837 to

1838, a series of rebellions occurred in Toronto and near Montreal. The rebels did not have enough support to overthrow the government, but they did prompt the British to make changes.

In 1840, Upper and Lower Canada became the Province of Canada. The concept of Responsible Government was introduced. This meant that leaders needed the support of a majority of elected representatives before making decisions, an important step toward a government that represented the people. It remains an essential part of Canada's government.

In 1867, Canada took another big step. Representatives from across Canada worked with representatives from Britain to form a new country. The Dominion of Canada was created, and it included four provinces: Ontario, Quebec, New Brunswick, and Nova Scotia. The country still was under the rule of the British king or queen. But for the first time, Canada would be self-governing. Each province would elect representatives to a Canadian parliament, which would be headed by the country's prime minister.

EXCLUDING IMMIGRANTS

The construction of the Canadian Pacific Railway brought together workers from many backgrounds, including many Chinese immigrants. The railway became a source of pride for Canadians, who saw it as uniting the large, diverse country. But when the construction was complete, the government enacted a divisive law called the Head Tax. The law discouraged the arrival of additional Chinese immigrants. Laws limiting immigration from China were in place from 1885 to 1947. Prime Minister Stephen Harper issued an official apology for the discriminatory policies in 2006.

EXPANDING WEST

The new country expanded quickly, claiming Manitoba, the Northwest Territories (which included present-day Alberta and Saskatchewan), British Columbia, Prince Edward Island, and Yukon. Construction began on the Canadian Pacific Railway, which would connect Montreal to the Pacific Coast. By 1885, the route was completed.

However, the country's expansion came at a price. When Canada began claiming territory, Indigenous peoples were not consulted. They did not have representation in the Canadian government. Also, settlers were bringing changes to the west, such as the destruction of the bison population, which changed Indigenous ways of life.

Métis leader Louis Riel led a series of rebellions in present-day Alberta and Saskatchewan. Métis people have mixed European and First Nations heritage. The rebels demanded that Métis and Indigenous land rights be respected. Instead of negotiating, the Canadian government sent troops to put down the rebellions. A series of bloody battles followed.

Eventually, the Métis and First Nations peoples signed treaties with the Canadian government. The government set up areas of land called reserves for the Indigenous peoples. In return for moving to the reserves, Indigenous peoples received government assistance for needs such as education and health care. However, in the years that followed, the government often failed to fulfill its treaty obligations.

In the late 1800s, immigration to western Canada increased. More than one million British people and one million Americans immigrated to Canada. Additionally, 170,000 Ukrainians,

115,000 Poles, and tens of thousands of people from Germany, France, Norway, and Sweden settled in the west.[4] With the increase in population, the provinces of Alberta and Saskatchewan were broken off from the Northwest Territories in 1905.

INTERNMENT

During both world wars, the Canadian government made the decision to intern, or detain, immigrants in the country. These people, identified as "enemy aliens," were from countries with which the British Empire was at war. During World War I, this included 8,500 immigrants from countries such as Ukraine, Germany, and Turkey. During World War II, around 24,000 people were interned, including about 21,000 Japanese people.[7] In 1988, the Canadian government apologized to Japanese Canadians interned during World War II and issued payments to survivors.

GOING TO WAR

When World War I (1914–1918) broke out, Canada had only a small army tasked with protecting its borders. But when the United Kingdom joined the war in 1914, Canada by extension did as well. More than 600,000 of the country's eight million people served in World War I. By the end of the war, 60,000 Canadians had died, with another 170,000 wounded.[5] The collective effort helped build a sense of national identity. Women's contributions overseas and at home, following decades of efforts, helped certain women gain the right to vote in federal elections in 1918.

During World War II (1939–1945), Canada again found itself at war in Europe. Canada joined the Allied powers of the United Kingdom, the United States, and the Soviet Union to fight against the Axis Powers of Germany, Italy, and Japan. Out of a population of 11.5 million Canadians, more than one million served in the war.[6] Canadians made key contributions to the effort. The Royal

MINI **BIO**

LOUIS RIEL

Louis Riel is a controversial figure in Canada's history. Riel was born in 1844 and grew up in the Red River Settlement in what is now Manitoba. The settlement was administered by the Hudson's Bay Company. It was also home to Métis people.

In 1869, the Métis learned that their land rights had been transferred to the government of Canada. Concerned about what this could mean for his people, Riel helped lead a rebellion. The Métis seized Upper Fort Garry, the region's administrative capital, and set up a provisional government. Riel negotiated directly with the federal government. The result was the Manitoba Act, which established Manitoba as a province and provided protection for French language rights.

In 1885, Riel attempted another uprising. This time, the attempt failed. Riel was tried, found guilty of treason, and executed at the age of 41. In the years that followed, many Canadians saw Riel and the Métis people as traitors. But many Métis and French-speaking Canadians viewed him as a hero for opposing unfair policies.

November 16 is Riel Day across the Métis homeland.

About 4,500 women served overseas in the Royal Canadian Army Medical Corps in World War II.[9]

Canadian Air Force helped the British win the Battle of Britain in 1940. At the Battle of Normandy in 1944, Canadian troops took one of the five beaches involved in the invasion of France. The Allied victory in World War II came at a high cost for Canada, with more than 44,000 Canadian soldiers killed.[8]

POSTWAR CHANGES

Wartime needs created a surge in Canadian manufacturing. After the war, Canada's economy boomed. Freeways and public transportation systems were built. Immigration continued, and the population grew. Strong labor unions pushed for better conditions for workers. Indigenous people and ethnic minorities gained expanded access to voting. On the international stage, Canada became a founding member of the United Nations and the North Atlantic Treaty Organization (NATO) military alliance.

But significant tensions remained. New economic development in western Canada brought the Canadian government increasingly into conflict with Indigenous ways of life. Conditions on reserves were poor. And populations at Indigenous residential schools were also at an all-time high. At these schools, children were forced to abandon their Indigenous heritage. They could not speak their languages or practice their traditions. Many were also physically mistreated, and some died. In the 1960s and 1970s, Indigenous activism increased. National organizations such

Conditions in residential schools were often cramped. Diseases spread easily.

as the Assembly of First Nations and the Native Council of Canada worked for improvements to education and economic development.

Tensions between French- and English-speaking citizens also rose. A movement called the Quiet Revolution pushed for more independence for French-speaking Quebec. Some people believed Quebec should separate from Canada entirely. The movement resulted in the Official Languages Act, which gave French and English equal status as official languages in Canada. In 1982, Canada took the final step toward becoming an independent nation. With the Constitution Act, Canada gained the right to make changes to its own constitution.

On July 1, 2021, people attended the Every Child Matters walk in Toronto. The event honored survivors of residential schools. People wore orange shirts in honor of the survivors.

TO THE PRESENT

The 1990s and early 2000s saw Canada become closer to the United States in both economic and military matters. In 1994, Canada, the United States, and Mexico signed the North American Free Trade Agreement (NAFTA), reducing barriers to trade between the countries. Following the September 11, 2001, terrorist attack against the United States, Canada joined the US-led Afghanistan War (2001–2014).

Domestically, groups within Canada continued to push for their rights. In 1992, the Inuit persuaded the Canadian government to acknowledge their rights to Arctic lands. The government gave the Inuit control of more than 135,000 square miles (350,000 sq km) of land.[10] This became the territory of Nunavut, which means "Our Land." In Nunavut, the Inuit have local self-government. From 2007 to 2015, the Truth and Reconciliation Commission operated. The commission was a project to inform all Canadians about what had happened in residential schools and to propose recommendations to advance the reconciliation process.

A disruption occurred in 2020, when COVID-19 reached Canada. The pandemic hit the country hard. Early on, the government imposed rules to try to stop the spread of the disease. Measures included mandatory masks, business closures, and social distancing. Canada's death rate from COVID-19 was significantly lower than that of the United States. But the government's policies divided Canadians. Canada suffered its greatest economic blow since the Great Depression of the 1930s. The disruptions caused by the pandemic also highlighted a number of ongoing issues in Canadian society, including wealth inequality, discrimination, and housing insecurity.

CHAPTER **FIVE**

PEOPLE AND CULTURE

Canada is a nation of immigrants. In Canada, the phrase "cultural mosaic" is often used to describe this mix of cultures. The phrase reflects an approach that embraces each culture as distinct. In 1988, this approach became enshrined into law. Canada passed the Canadian Multiculturalism Act, the world's first multiculturalism policy. The act acknowledged the multicultural history of the country and provided funds to promote cultural exchange.

Today, Canadians represent more than 450 ethnic or cultural origins. The top nations of origin are England at 15 percent, Scotland at 12 percent, Ireland at 12 percent, and France at 11 percent. Approximately 2 percent

Granville Island Public Market is an indoor market in Vancouver. Visitors can purchase food and goods from many of the cultures that make up Canada.

report Indigenous heritage.[1] Significant numbers of Canadians also have roots in Germany, Italy, Ukraine, China, and India.

About two-thirds of Canadians are religious. Christianity is the most common religion, with Christians making up 53 percent of the population. Of this group, more than half are Roman Catholic. Around 5 percent of Canadians are Muslim, 2 percent are Hindu, and 2 percent are Sikh.[2]

Canadians speak more than 200 languages. The Canadian government recognizes both French and English as official languages. This means people can interact with the federal government in either language. About 87 percent of Canadians speak English, and about 29 percent speak French, with most French speakers living in Quebec.[3] About 18 percent of Canadians speak both English and French.[4]

One-quarter of Canadians have a first language that is not English or French. The most common of these are Mandarin Chinese and Punjabi, both of which have more than half a million speakers. Spanish, Arabic, and Tagalog are other commonly spoken languages.[5]

CANADIAN HOLIDAYS

Uniquely Canadian holidays include Canada Day on July 1, which marks the unification of the provinces, and the National Day for Truth and Reconciliation on September 30, which remembers victims of Canadian residential schools. Christian holidays such as Christmas on December 25 and Easter in March or April are also celebrated nationwide. Muslims, Jews, Hindus, Buddhists, and other religious minorities have the right to take their holy days off work. Many Canadians also celebrate holidays such as Thanksgiving in October, Halloween on October 31, Valentine's Day on February 14, and Saint Patrick's Day on March 17.

In 2019, the Indigenous Languages Act passed. The act's goal was to promote and revitalize the use of Indigenous languages across Canada. Currently, more than 70 different Indigenous languages are spoken, with Cree languages and the Inuit language of Inuktitut being the most common.[6]

FIRST NATIONS, INUIT, AND MÉTIS

Indigenous peoples are those who lived in what is now Canada before European settlers arrived. Today, three broad groups are recognized. These are First Nations, Inuit, and Métis.

First Nations describes most Indigenous nations in Canada who are not Métis or Inuit. First Nations encompasses more than 50 nations.[7] About 38 percent of First Nations people live on reserves.[8] In these areas, First Nations people form their own governments and practice their own cultures. Cultural expression for First Nations people may take the form of ceremonies, traditional ways of life, and artistic pursuits. Many contemporary First Nations visual artists have found popular success. Some adapt traditional forms, and others blend Western influences with more personal subject matter.

Inuit means "the people" and refers to the Indigenous nations historically located in the Arctic. Inuit make up a majority of the population in Nunavut. In Nunavut, almost all Inuit people can still speak Inuktitut. Traditional food sources such as whales, seals, caribou, and fish remain important to the Inuit. But they also buy foods shipped from other regions. While some Inuit continue to work as hunters, many others work in mining, tourism, and other jobs.

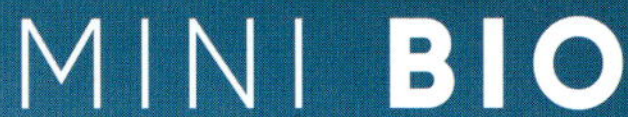

BILL REID

Bill Reid was one of Canada's most well-known First Nations artists. Reid was born in 1920 to a Haida mother and Scottish-American father, but he did not know of his Indigenous heritage until his teenage years. Later, he studied jewelry and engraving and began to learn about Haida arts. He became widely known for his massive sculptures reminiscent of the totem poles carved by the Haida.

One of Reid's most famous works is a bronze statue of an orca. It sits outside the Vancouver Aquarium. Another is *The Spirit of Haida Gwaii*, located outside the Canadian Embassy in Washington, DC.

In addition to his artwork, Reid advocated for Indigenous rights in Canada. While working on *The Spirit of Haida Gwaii*, he paused to protest logging occurring on the islands of Haida Gwaii, which are near British Columbia. At the time of his death in 1998, Reid was credited with bringing about a revival of northwestern coast Indigenous arts.

Bill Reid's orca was installed at the Vancouver Aquarium in 1984.

Métis refers to people with combined Indigenous and European heritage and cultural practices, with origins rooted in the southern prairies. Métis culture reflects these influences. Michif-Cree, for example, is a Métis language that combines French nouns with Cree sentence structures. Métis music and dance includes European-style fiddling with the fast-paced footwork from First Nations dance and beats common in First Nations drumming.

DISTINCT CITIES

Canadian cities are important centers of Canadian culture. About 75 percent of Canadians live in cities of at least 100,000 people.[9] The character of each city reflects the history of the place as well as the people who live there.

Quebec City is the capital of Quebec and the heart of French-Canadian culture. Its Old Quebec district is a UNESCO World Heritage site. The cobblestone square of Place-Royale is lined with buildings dating to the late 1600s. Elsewhere, grand buildings such as the Château Frontenac bring to mind the grandeur of centuries-old European buildings.

Victoria, British Columbia, displays a distinct British influence. The city began as a trading post for the Hudson's Bay Company. Eventually, the settlement became so successful it was named the capital of British Columbia. Today, massive gardens and ornate architecture remind visitors of the nation's British roots.

Elsewhere, cultural expression takes the form of festivals. Calgary is located where the prairie meets the Rocky Mountains. In the 1800s, it became the heart of Canada's cattle industry.

The Calgary Stampede includes saddle bronc competitions, in which riders try to stay on a bucking horse for eight seconds.

Each July, the colorful ten-day Calgary Stampede celebrates this history, featuring a large outdoor rodeo with events such as barrel racing, bull riding, and saddle bronc riding. It also includes concerts, parades, and other festivities.

In October, the Celtic Colours International Festival in Nova Scotia observes the province's Scottish influences. Scots were among the first settlers in the region, and today more than a quarter of Nova Scotians have Scottish heritage. The festival celebrates this history with nine days of music, dance, and storytelling.

FOOD

Canadian food also expresses the country's historical and cultural influences. One major contributor is Indigenous cuisines, which developed over millennia and are rooted in local ingredients. Recipes and ingredients such as salmon, bison meat, and wild berries have made important contributions to Canadian cuisine. So have Indigenous ways of preserving foods, such as smoking, drying, and roasting.

European influences have also added flavor to Canada's cuisine. The French introduced dishes such as tourtière, a savory meat pie. The English added foods such as roast beef and puddings. Distinctly Canadian dishes have also emerged. Poutine, a popular snack consisting of cheese curds, fries, and gravy, evolved over decades in the unique conditions of French Quebec. Ginger beef, which is beef fried in candied sweet ginger sauce, was the result of Chinese influences. Middle Eastern culinary influences are found in *donair*, a kebab served with a sauce made of condensed milk, vinegar, and sugar.

Almost 47 percent of Toronto residents were born in another country.[10]

Toronto, the largest and most diverse city in Canada, is the nation's culinary capital. This is reflected in its foods. The city is a popular destination for foodies seeking Cantonese dim sum, Vietnamese pho, and Caribbean jerk chicken.

THE ARTS

Because Canadians are spread over such vast areas, distinctly Canadian forms of art outside of Indigenous art were slow to develop. In 1951, the government published the Massey Report. It warned that Canadian culture was at risk of being overwhelmed by US culture. The government declared that mass media, such as TV shows, movies, books, and magazines, needed

Canadian content. The Canadian Broadcasting Corporation, which had a national radio network, was put in charge of television. In 1957, the Canada Council for the Arts was established, which awarded grants to writers, artists, and theaters.

The investment paid off. In the postwar boom, people had money to spend on entertainment. Thriving arts scenes developed in cities. Symphony orchestras in Toronto and Montreal became internationally recognized. Toronto, Montreal, and Vancouver developed opera seasons, and three top-ranking ballet companies are now found in Canada.

Canada also has a vibrant pop and rock music heritage. Many Canadian artists found major success in the massive US market. Famous Canadian artists who have achieved international success include Neil Young, Joni Mitchell, and Leonard Cohen. More recently, artists such as Justin Bieber, Carly Rae Jepsen, and Drake have risen to fame.

A number of comedy actors got their start in Toronto in the 1970s, including eventual Hollywood stars Dan Aykroyd, Catherine O'Hara, John Candy, Martin Short, and Jim Carrey.

THE GROUP OF SEVEN

Painting was an art form in which Canadians excelled in the early 1900s. Following the formation of a Canadian nation in 1867, many artists worked to develop a particular Canadian style. In 1920, a group of Toronto artists chose to focus on landscapes, emphasizing Canada's natural beauty. They became known as the Group of Seven. Artist Tom Thomson was one of their major influences. Each year, he spent time immersed in nature as a woodsman or guide, which inspired his art.

While English-Canadian television and filmmaking struggled to compete against Hollywood, French-Canadian television and films thrived, offering programming that wasn't available elsewhere. Over time, Canada became a destination for foreign filmmakers thanks to lower costs and a talented filmmaking workforce.

SPORTS

Canada's national winter sport is ice hockey, which was created in Canada in the 1800s. The sport is a popular pastime during Canada's long winters. The country has produced many of the world's top players, including Wayne Gretzky, Gordie Howe, Mario Lemieux, Sidney Crosby, and Hayley Wickenheiser. The men's national team has a record nine Olympic gold medals and 28 world championships.[11] The women's national team also leads the way with five Olympic gold medals and 13 world championships.[12]

Carly Rae Jepsen was born in Mission, British Columbia, in 1985.

Wayne Gretzky is considered the greatest hockey player of all time, and many of his records still stood into the 2020s, including his record of 50 goals in 39 games.

Lacrosse is the country's national summer sport and the oldest organized sport in North America. Haudenosaunee people have played a version of the game for hundreds of years. Today, Canada's national outdoor lacrosse teams are among the top teams in the world. The men's team has three championships and seven runner-up titles.[13] The women's team has medaled five times.[14] A professional indoor league, the National Lacrosse League, features six Canadian teams and eight US teams.

Other popular spectator sports include basketball, baseball, soccer, and football. Toronto represents Canadian cities in the National Basketball Association with the Raptors and in Major League Baseball with the Blue Jays. Meanwhile, following an Olympic gold medal for the women's soccer team in 2020, soccer has become the most popular sport among young athletes.

CANADIAN COMEDY

Many Canadian comedians and comic actors have found success in the United States. One theory about this is that Canadians share much of the same culture as Americans but also feel outside it, allowing them to offer a humorous perspective. *Saturday Night Live*, created by Canadian Lorne Michaels, is one example, as the show often pokes fun at American pop culture and politics. Regardless of the reason, offbeat Canadian actors, including Seth Rogen, Samantha Bee, and Michael Cera, continue to find success in American media.

CHAPTER **SIX**

POLITICS

Since 1931, Canada has been part of the British Commonwealth. Today, this group consists of more than 50 nations, most of which have past connections to the British Empire.[1] Along with 13 other commonwealth countries, Canada continues to recognize the British monarch as its head of state.[2]

The monarch's duties in Canada are carried out by a representative. This person is known as the governor general. The governor general's role in Canadian politics is mostly ceremonial.

The day-to-day governing of the country is left up to the prime minister, the legislature, and the judicial system. But in times of emergency, Canada's constitution grants the governor general the ability to step in. For example, if a leader refuses to leave office after losing an election, the governor general can

Canada's government meets in buildings on Parliament Hill in Ottawa, Ontario. Visitors can take guided tours of these buildings, which include the Senate of Canada Building and the House of Commons.

dismiss the leader and call for elections. However, this has never happened in Canada's history.

THE EXECUTIVE BRANCH

Like the United Kingdom and many other commonwealth nations, Canada's federal government is a parliamentary democracy. In this system, people do not vote for an individual, such as a president, to lead the country. They vote for politicians to represent them in Parliament, the country's legislature. The political party that gets the most seats in Parliament becomes the ruling party. The ruling party forms the executive branch of the government. This branch can develop policies and can introduce bills to the legislature.

Party members elect a leader. The leader of the ruling party becomes the prime minister. Like the president in the United States, the prime minister of Canada is the head of government. This person often represents the nation in policy discussions with foreign leaders. The prime minister decides what the government's agenda should be.

CANADA'S COAT OF ARMS

One of Canada's official symbols is its coat of arms, or national crest. The coat of arms appears on Canadian passports and official government publications. The crest draws on Canada's European connections, featuring a lion and a unicorn representing England and Scotland. On a shield between them are three fleurs-de-lis, a common symbol of France. One of Canada's national mottoes, "They Desire a Better Country," appears in Latin, representing the nation's immigrants. Critics of the symbol argue that the crest should be redone to acknowledge Indigenous peoples.

To carry out the agenda, the prime minister selects a cabinet of politicians known as ministers. Each minister is in charge of a different area of government, such as health, foreign affairs, and transportation. There is no set number for ministers, but usually there are around three dozen.

Ministers develop policies within each area. Because ministers are also members of Parliament, they introduce bills they hope to turn into law. Ministers report to Parliament about the departments they oversee.

THE LEGISLATIVE BRANCH

The legislative branch is tasked with creating laws. The federal legislature consists of the two houses of Parliament, which are the Senate and the House of Commons. For a law to be passed, it must be adopted by both houses.

Justin Trudeau became prime minister in 2015. He continued to hold that position into the mid-2020s.

The governor general sits on the Monarch's Throne in the Senate. This throne represents the British Crown in Senate meetings, which are called sittings.

The House of Commons is made of more than 300 members of Parliament (MPs), who are elected to represent the districts of the country.[3] The number of representatives from each province is based on population. MPs introduce bills, discuss legislation, and suggest amendments to bills from the Senate.

The Senate has 105 members. Each region has a set number of senators. The four major regions—the eastern coast provinces, Ontario, Quebec, and the western provinces—each have 24 senators. The Northern Territories and Newfoundland and Labrador are represented by the remaining nine senators. This distribution is meant to ensure that the interests of the whole country, not just the most populous regions, are represented in discussions about proposed laws.

Senators serve similar roles to MPs. But rather than being elected, they are appointed by the prime minister. Because of this, senators have some limits on their powers. For example, they cannot introduce bills that propose new spending of taxpayer dollars. Senators can slow down the lawmaking process by proposing amendments.

Every four years, an election is held. The people may vote for the same party to form the next government. Or they may vote for a new party to take power. If a ruling party becomes unpopular before the next regular election, MPs may hold a vote of confidence. A vote of confidence measures whether the party still has majority support in Parliament. If a majority of MPs vote against the ruling party, Parliament is dissolved. A nationwide election takes place to elect a new government. Throughout history, the government of Canada has been dissolved early six times because of votes from the House.

THE JUDICIAL BRANCH

The judicial system in Canada stands independent from the executive and legislative branches. The role of the judiciary is to interpret and apply the laws and the constitution. It is divided into federal and provincial courts. Judges on federal courts and higher provincial courts are appointed by the prime minister.

The highest court is the Supreme Court of Canada. Judges serve until they are 75 years old, when they are required to retire. Parliament has the right to remove a federal judge in case of poor behavior, but it has never done so.

Diversity in the courts has been a source of controversy. For the Supreme Court's first 147 years of existence, every judge was white. This changed in 2021, with the appointment of the first justice of color. A year later, the first Indigenous justice was appointed.

LOCAL GOVERNMENT

Responsibility for lawmaking in Canada is shared by federal, provincial, and local governments. Provinces have their own legislative, executive, and judicial systems. These mirror the federal system.

Each province has a lieutenant governor, who represents the British monarch's authority and performs a largely ceremonial role. The provinces hold elections for a single-chamber legislative assembly, and the winning party forms a government. The sparsely populated territories are administered by the federal government but practice self-government at the local level.

On special occasions, Canada's Supreme Court judges wear red robes lined with white fur, a style that dates back to 1300s England.

POLITICAL PARTIES

Canada's party system is hierarchical. A single leader at the top sets the party's policy agenda and takes stances on the issues of the day. Other federal and provincial politicians within the party are expected to support and endorse the leader's agenda. They can be expelled for not doing so.

While the party with the most representatives forms the federal government, the party with the second most representatives forms the official opposition. The leader of the official opposition

In Canada, ballots can be collected in boxes and counted by hand. Other times, automated counters are used.

sits across from the prime minister in Parliament. The opposition party's role is that of a watchdog, ensuring that the prime minister and ruling party consider opposing views. There are two major parties in Canada, but several smaller parties are also active. Those that earn 12 or more seats in the House of Commons receive funding, with the goal of increasing the diversity of the debate in Parliament.[4]

The Liberal Party is the country's oldest and most successful party. Pierre Trudeau, who served as prime minister from 1968 to 1979 and from 1980 to 1984, is one of the party's most significant figures. Trudeau aimed to create a "Just Society" that supported marginalized people. While he was of French descent, he was against the Quiet Revolution, which pushed for Quebec's independence. Trudeau believed a stronger federal government would help unite the country and support its citizens.

THE PEOPLE'S PARTY

In 2018, prominent MP Maxime Bernier left the Conservative Party to create a new party, the People's Party of Canada (PPC). The PPC is considered more conservative than the Conservative Party. The party pushes for greatly reducing immigration in order to maintain the country's cultural character. To help the economy, the PPC supports withdrawing from the Paris Agreement climate change treaty and expanding the country's oil and gas industries. In 2021, the party found particular support for its opposition to the Trudeau government's COVID-19 policies. While the party did not gain any seats in Parliament, it received 5 percent of the vote.[5]

The Liberal Party continues to support socially progressive ideas. Pierre Trudeau's son, Justin Trudeau, became prime minister in 2015. Under the younger Trudeau, the Liberal Party has supported abortion access, LGBTQ rights, and expansive immigration. The party is more skeptical of big-government solutions, or those that involve extensive government spending, than it was in the past.

The Conservative Party of Canada is the nation's second-largest party. The Canadian conservative movement traces its roots to the Tories of the 1800s. This group of Canadians was loyal to British rule, practiced Protestantism, and valued English culture. Under Brian Mulroney, who was prime minister from 1984 to 1993, the conservative focus shifted to shrinking the size of the federal government and increasing trade.

The Conservative Party continues to favor these policies in the form of lower taxes and less government regulation of businesses, as well as a strong military. In 2022, Pierre Poilievre became the party leader. Poilievre is known for his criticism of the media and elite institutions, which he sees as disconnected from everyday Canadians.

Other political parties include the New Democratic Party (NDP), the Bloc Québécois party, and the Green Party. The NDP began as a socialist party during the Great Depression. It continues to advocate for close government involvement in the economy as well as higher taxes for the wealthy. The NDP has never elected a prime minister, but it has played a significant role in supporting Canada's pension and national health-care systems.

The Bloc Québécois formed in 1990 to support Quebec independence. Today, it is the third-largest party in Parliament and continues to advocate exclusively for Quebecois interests. However, because it runs candidates only in Quebec, it can never form a government.

The Green Party of Canada began in the 1980s and initially ran exclusively on environmental issues. While this remains a central focus, Greens today also advocate for reforms to the Canadian electoral system, among other issues. The party has had little success nationally but is among the most popular parties at the provincial level.

MILITARY AND DEFENSE

The Canadian military consists of three separate branches: the Canadian Army, Royal Canadian Navy, and Royal Canadian Air Force. These branches are collectively headed by the chief of the defense staff, who reports directly to the prime minister. This unified military structure allows for joint training of recruits and for commanding officers to move from branch to branch. The military

About 5,000 Canadian Rangers, part of the Canadian Army Reserve, help patrol Canada's vast Arctic shores.[6]

includes about 70,000 active-duty members.[7] The air force has more than 350 aircraft.[8] In 2022, Canada expanded the Royal Canadian Air Force to include a space division.

With the exception of the world wars, Canada's military has historically been a small, lightly funded force. This is due in part to its close ties with the United States, whose military greatly expanded during the Cold War (1947–1991). Canada collaborates militarily with the United States as part of the North American Aerospace Defense Command (NORAD) and with the other nations in NATO.

Canada is among the lowest military spenders in the NATO alliance. The issue of military spending remains a controversial political issue in the country. Conservatives usually support a stronger military, while liberals generally advocate for peacekeeping and humanitarian causes, such as making sure ceasefire agreements are honored, clearing landmines, and helping refugees.

CANADIANS IN SPACE

In addition to its military space activities, Canada has the civilian-led Canadian Space Agency (CSA), which began in 1989. The CSA trains astronauts, develops satellites, and advances space research and technology. The agency collaborates with other nations to support the International Space Station (ISS). In 2001, Canada contributed the Canadarm2, a large arm used to move supplies, make repairs, and dock space shuttles to the station. In 2019, the agency agreed to partner on the US-led Lunar Gateway program, which aims to create a space station that will orbit the moon.

CHAPTER **SEVEN**

ECONOMICS

Throughout its history, the Canadian economy has undergone major shifts in response to changing political, cultural, and economic demands. In the early days of colonization, the economic system consisted of a simple fur trade. Hunters collected and sold animal skins to large fur companies. These companies used the profits from selling the furs to buy up more land.

As Europeans moved across the continent, they discovered new possibilities for industry. Resources such as coal, iron, gold, and silver were discovered on the Canadian Shield. The plains offered massive lands that could be turned into grain fields and pastures for raising meat and dairy livestock. Goods were shipped to Britain and France. And as Canada took steps toward independence, trade with the United States increased.

Tourists visit both Canada's cities and its natural areas. They put tens of billions of dollars into the Canadian economy each year.

The Pacific Mills paper mill in British Columbia made products such as wallpaper in the early 1900s.

In the late 1800s and early 1900s, advances in technology meant that machines replaced human labor in many industries, allowing for faster production of goods. Agriculture became more efficient. Raw materials could be more easily turned into finished products. Instead of exporting goods such as lumber, coal, and iron, Canadians began producing products such as paper, cloth, and steel. New commodities were also traded, including oil and natural gas.

After World War II, the economy underwent another change. The government charged higher taxes and channeled money toward social services, including the funding of universities. More Canadians invested in education, allowing them to demand higher wages. By the 1980s, a majority of Canadian workers held white-collar jobs, which usually take place in offices and involve administrative or managerial work.

In 1994, Canada signed on to NAFTA. This agreement lowered trade barriers with the United States and Mexico. As these barriers came down, some companies moved manufacturing

CANADA'S CURRENCY

Since 1858, Canada has used the Canadian dollar (CAD) as its currency. The Royal Canadian Mint issues banknotes, which range from five dollars to $100. Coins include quarters, dimes, and nickels as well as one- and two-dollar coins. Pennies are still used but have not been minted since 2012. The one-dollar coin is called a Loonie because it features the loon, a bird found throughout most of Canada. The two-dollar coin is known as the Twoonie or Toonie. Due to Canada's economic and political stability, the Canadian dollar is among the top currencies for the world's central banks to hold in reserve.

to countries where the cost of labor was lower. In 2020, NAFTA was replaced with the United States–Mexico–Canada Agreement (USMCA). The new agreement made some changes to help spur manufacturing but largely kept NAFTA's policies in place.

THE ECONOMY TODAY

Canada's gross domestic product (GDP) in 2023 was $2.1 trillion.[1] Many industries contribute. The service sector employs 75 percent of the Canadian workforce.[2] Service jobs focus on working with or for people rather than on producing goods. One subsector includes trade workers such as carpenters and computer repair technicians. Other subsectors include finance, education, food and retail, and the arts. Government work also falls into the service sector. The largest employer in Canada is the Canadian government, which provides jobs in areas such as health care.

The fastest-growing part of the Canadian service sector is tourism. Canada is a leading destination for US travelers, attracting more than 21 million Americans per year.[3] The country attracts large numbers of British, French, Mexican, and Indian tourists as well.

Canada produced more than ten million gallons (38 million L) of maple syrup in 2023.[6]

About 9 percent of Canada's labor force works in manufacturing.[4] Ontario and Quebec are home to more than 75 percent of these jobs, many of which are in the automotive sector.[5] In British Columbia, timber and paper remain important manufactured goods. Other Canadian goods include chemicals, machinery, and electronics.

Agriculture makes up about 3 percent of Canada's labor force but remains an important part of the country's economy.[7] Canada is among the world's top producers of wheat and canola. The climate in eastern Canada makes the region perfect for harvesting sugar maple sap, and globally Canada is the world's leading producer of maple products. The rainy, fast-growing forests of British Columbia make the region particularly good for forestry. Canada is the top exporter of wood pulp, which is used to make tissues, books, and packaging.

Canada has rich fishing grounds and is among the top fish exporters. On the eastern coast, the continental shelf extends far into the ocean, allowing a large, shallow area for fish such as flounder, herring, and tuna to be caught. On the western coast, coastal streams are filled with salmon.

Canada is rich in minerals. Gold can be found on the Canadian Shield. Silver and copper are mined in the Western Cordillera. The Interior Plains hold coal, uranium, and potash, a mineral used to make fertilizer. The Northwest Territories are home to Canada's diamond industry, known for producing high-quality gems. The price of minerals greatly affects mining activities. If prices increase, new mines open. If prices drop, mines may be shuttered.

Canada also exports energy. It has about one-sixth of the world's hydroelectric capacity, and

THE SUDBURY BASIN

One of the richest areas for mining in Canada is the Sudbury Basin in Ontario. The basin is 37 miles (60 km) wide and was formed approximately 1.9 billion years ago when a massive meteor struck Earth.[8] Fragments from the impact have been found hundreds of miles away. The collision punctured Earth's crust, bringing up molten material from deep beneath the surface. As a result, the crater became rich in rare metals such as gold, nickel, copper, cobalt, and platinum.

Canada has more than 630 large hydroelectric dams, including some in Ottawa.

three-fifths of the country's energy comes from hydroelectric sources.[9] The country has plenty of electricity. It also has more than enough natural gas. As a result, it sends oil and gas produced in Alberta south to the United States.

INFRASTRUCTURE

Infrastructure has always been key to Canada's growth and success. Recognizing the importance of a well-connected nation, the Canadian government has played a major role in infrastructure development. In some cases, this has meant giving subsidies to companies to build railways and roads. Other times, the government has nationalized transportation companies, which means it takes over the companies to ensure effective services. It has also established Crown corporations, which are state-owned businesses that operate like private companies.

In cities, buses are the most common form of transport. But trains, subways, light-rail, and bikes are also common options in Canadian cities. Major cities are connected via road, rail, water, and air transport. Along the Pacific Coast, ferries are commonly used to bring people to cities such as Victoria, which is located on Vancouver Island. VIA Rail Canada provides passenger rail services across the country. The most efficient way for people to move across Canada is by air. The country has several international airports. Planes and helicopters are the only ways to reach the most isolated places, such as Inuit settlements in the north.

For transporting goods, Canadians use rails, water, roads, air, and pipelines. The Saint Lawrence Seaway is a vital shipping system. The seaway features natural riverways, human-made canals, and a series of locks, allowing massive ships to travel from the Atlantic Coast to Lake Superior.

CROWN CORPORATIONS

Canada has long used Crown corporations to provide services the government believes are in the public's interest but which corporations may not be willing to perform. Transportation services are one example. Cross-country passenger railways and ferry services to remote islands are expensive to provide. Crown corporations such as VIA Rail Canada and Marine Atlantic Incorporated ensure these services remain available to Canadians. Other Crown corporations include the Canada Post, which handles the mail, and the Canadian Broadcasting Corporation, which provides distinctly Canadian media.

Because the seaway connects the Great Lakes, it also fosters extensive trade between the United States and Canada.

TRADE WITH THE UNITED STATES

Canada's largest trading partner is the United States. More than 75 percent of Canadian trade happens with its neighbor to the south.[10] The most valuable goods Canada sends to the United States include energy resources such as oil, chemical fuels, electricity, and natural gas. Raw natural resources such as aluminum, nickel, gold, and iron ore are popular exports too. From the United States, Canada imports food, chemicals, electronics, and entertainment products.

The two countries also share a supply chain. The most significant example of this is in the auto industry, where parts move back and forth between Ontario and the state of Michigan. This joint auto industry builds more than one-quarter of the cars produced in North America.[11]

Some Canadians worry about the close economic ties between the two countries. Around 50 percent of direct foreign investment in Canada is held by Americans.[12] Much of this investment comes in the form of US corporations expanding into Canada. These companies produce jobs for Canadians. However, they can also keep Canadian-owned companies from developing.

To protect certain industries, Canada limits the amount of foreign investment in areas such as telecommunications, energy, national defense, and culture. International relationships can change. For this reason, having Canadian-owned businesses in these areas helps ensure Canadians continue to have access to the products.

In 2022, more than 198 million short tons (180 million metric tons) of goods were shipped via the Saint Lawrence Seaway.

In addition to the United States, Canada trades with the European Union, China, and Mexico. Together, these partners represent about 20 percent of Canadian trade.[13] Canada also has free trade agreements with much of Latin America, Middle Eastern countries such as Israel and Jordan, and non–European Union countries including Iceland, Norway, and Switzerland.

CHAPTER **EIGHT**

CANADA TODAY

Canada ranks well in several quality-of-life indicators. Life expectancy is high, with the average Canadian living beyond age 80.[1] The median salary of workers is high. Crime is relatively low, with the country ranking 11 out of 163 countries in terms of safety.[2] In addition to a high standard of living and long life expectancy, Canadian citizens have universal access to health care. Necessary medical care is free at the point of service for all Canadians.

Canada also has a strong social safety net. The Canadian Pension Plan and Old Age Security program help ensure citizens have income after the retirement age of 65. Employment insurance helps people transition after losing a job. It also pays parents

Many Canadians enjoy getting outdoors year-round, playing winter sports for fun with family and friends or as part of organized teams.

Classes help immigrants to Canada learn skills to aid them in getting jobs in their new home.

following the birth or adoption of a child. Maternity leave lasts 15 weeks, and parental leave can last up to 69 weeks.[3] Canada's social safety net is funded by Canadian tax dollars. Canadians pay similar percentages of personal income taxes compared with people in the United States.

With a population of about 39 million—roughly the population of California—the country is considered underpopulated.[4] But Canada's population continues to grow and is expected to surpass 50 million in the 2070s.[5] Canada's birth rate has been steadily declining, but the country has made up for this by welcoming more immigrants. The nation's net migration rate, or the overall population increase due to immigration, is among the highest in the world.

LGBTQ RIGHTS IN CANADA

Since the 1960s, LGBTQ Canadians have seen slow but steady gains in rights. In the 1990s, Canada lifted military restrictions on gay and lesbian soldiers and began to allow same-sex adoption. In 2005, it became the fourth country to legalize same-sex marriage. In 2017, Bill C-16 updated the Canadian Human Rights Act to include gender identity and gender expression as prohibited grounds for discrimination. And in 2022, the country banned conversion therapy, or the forced changing of someone's gender identity or sexuality. Indigenous people who are two-spirit—those who embody masculine and feminine traits—are also covered by these laws.

DAILY LIFE AND SOCIAL ATTITUDES

Daily life in Canada varies significantly from place to place. Particularly in cities, routines are similar to those of US cities. Breakfast tends to be eaten first thing in the morning. Common breakfast foods include eggs, sausage, bacon, fried potatoes, and French toast with syrup. Lunch also tends to be a light meal. Usually eaten around noon, it often consists of sandwiches, soups, or salads. Dinner tends to be the largest and most well-prepared meal of the day.

When interacting in public, Canadians tend to be informal. Even in the workplace, where there are clear hierarchies, it's expected that people will be treated equally. This politeness extends to conversation. Being boastful about class or education status is frowned upon. Rather, Canadians tend to portray themselves as self-deprecating and deferential to others in public.

Social attitudes on controversial topics are relatively permissive in Canada. Activities such as gambling and the use of alcohol and marijuana are legal. Abortion is permitted with few restrictions. Gun ownership is high, but many models of assault-style firearms are prohibited. In 2022, the government placed a freeze on the sale of handguns.

EDUCATION

Education is a commonly shared value in Canada. The country is among the world leaders in adults with post-secondary degrees. School is required for students from roughly age five to 18. Most children begin with one or two years of kindergarten before entering elementary school at age six or seven. At about age 14, children begin a four-year secondary school, or high school.

Most primary and secondary schools in Canada are publicly funded by provincial governments. Public French immersion schools are offered throughout the English-speaking provinces. Meanwhile, in French-speaking Quebec, English schools are also popular. In all, more

High school students in Canada have opportunities to attend workshops at colleges and universities to help them learn additional skills and decide on a career.

Canadians have a 99 percent literacy rate.[9]

than 90 percent of students attend public schools. Schools run by Indigenous peoples are also funded by the government, but Indigenous authorities make decisions about curriculum, staffing, and language of instruction. About 7.5 percent of students attend private schools, and 1.5 percent are schooled at home.[6]

After graduating high school, many Canadian teens enroll in postsecondary education. *College* in Canada refers to schools focused on vocational training. *University* is used to describe schools that grant advanced degrees. It's common for Canadians to attend a college before enrolling in a university.

Canada has more than 75 degree-granting institutions and more than 200 community colleges.[7] Most schools are government funded, with tuition prices considerably lower than those in the United States. English is the most common language of instruction at universities. However, there are several French-language and bilingual schools. Top Canadian universities include the University of Toronto, the University of British Columbia, and McGill University. Each ranks among the top 100 universities in the world.[8]

SPORTS AND LEISURE

Outside of school, Canadian teens are expected to contribute to household chores, such as washing dishes and shoveling snow. Volunteering is also common. Some provinces have requirements that teens must volunteer for a specific amount of time to graduate. Working a part-time job is also common. Children younger than 18 may work under certain conditions. Most non-adult workers have jobs in retail, in fast food, or on family farms.

Many teens spend their leisure time socializing with friends, watching TV, or playing video games. Extracurricular programs to suit all interests are offered by communities and schools. Sports such as soccer, hockey, basketball, baseball, and swimming are common. So are outdoor activities such as hiking, fishing, boating, skiing, and snowboarding.

MEGA MALL

The West Edmonton Mall is the top tourist destination in Alberta, attracting more than 30 million visitors per year. The mall is among the largest in the world and is comparable in size to a small city. It is home to more than 800 stores, two hotels, and more than 100 restaurants.[10] It also includes an amusement park, a water park, indoor bungee jumping, a hockey rink, and an accredited zoo. Located in one of Canada's coldest large cities, the mall provides a climate-controlled escape all year long.

For vacation, Canadian families take advantage of the diverse array of natural sites their country has to offer. Banff National Park receives millions of visitors each year. In southern Alberta, the Canadian Badlands are another popular destination. The scenic, hilly landscape has been the site of many significant fossil discoveries. And the town of Drumheller is often called the dinosaur capital of the world.

In the winter, ski trips are common. Located in the Coast Mountains, Whistler offers alpine views and skiing for all ages. To the east, Le Massif de Charlevoix ski resort is just an hour's drive

Together, Whistler and its neighboring mountain Blackcomb have more than 200 runs for skiers and snowboarders to enjoy.

from Quebec City. With the Saint Lawrence River running along the base of the mountain, skiers can spot humpback and beluga whales from the slopes.

ISSUES TODAY

Economic issues are among the top problems facing Canada today. The COVID-19 pandemic disrupted international supply chains, causing inflated prices for some items. Demand for other items increased significantly, causing companies to raise prices. The rising prices for many goods and services was a continuation of a long-term trend in Canada. While the rate of inflation has slowed after the early pandemic, Canadians continue to struggle. Many Canadians have reported that rising prices are affecting their ability to pay for day-to-day expenses.

The cost of housing has also gone up considerably. For many Canadians, particularly those in large cities, buying a home seems out of reach. Between 2005 and 2022, Canadian housing prices more than doubled. This increase is due to a lack of housing supply in cities to accommodate growing populations. In 2022, the government invested heavily in housing, hoping to double the number of homes built each year. However, a construction labor shortage has made it difficult

A POOL OF OIL

Alberta is home to the world's third-largest oil reserves. These reserves are located in tar sands, which are areas of land covered by a mix of sand, water, clay, and a dense form of oil called bitumen. Extracting the oil is a difficult process and emits about three times more pollution than pumping conventional crude oil. In order to meet both its climate and economic goals, Canada plans to reduce emissions in the oil extraction process and continue production. Critics are skeptical that the government will be able to meet its targets. Some argue for shifting away from the oil industry completely.

for the nation to meet its goals. Due in part to these economic trends, some aspects of Canadian family and social life are changing. Young people are delaying leaving their parents' homes, buying homes of their own, and starting families.

Canadians' economic concerns are also tied to their concerns about climate change. Canada is known for its beautiful natural scenery and wildlife, and most Canadians deeply value the preservation of the country's lands. But the nation is a top emitter of greenhouse gases, which trap heat in the atmosphere. The effects of climate change can be seen in the increasing occurrence of flooding, wildfires, and weather-related emergencies. However, reducing the country's production of oil, gas, and coal comes with an economic cost.

In 2023, Canada's energy sector made up about 10 percent of the country's GDP. The sector directly employed nearly 300,000 people.[11] Because of the sector's size, moving quickly away from current forms of energy production could cause additional economic hardship for Canadians. Meeting the immediate needs of Canadians and the long-term needs of the environment remains a difficult balancing act for the government.

Canada's 2024 wildfire season was its sixth worst in the past 50 years.

Immigration, which is part of Canada's multicultural identity, is also a controversial issue. On one hand, the country relies on immigration to supplement the nation's low birth rate and to keep the economy growing. But in the midst of a housing crisis and inflated prices, about 60 percent of Canadians polled in 2024 said immigration is too high.[12]

In 2024, the Canadian government announced it would reduce immigration levels in the coming years. Liberal Party leader Justin Trudeau and Conservative Party leader Pierre Poilievre

Indigenous people in Canada gather to raise awareness of injustices toward their people. There is a higher rate of missing and murdered Indigenous women and girls than for other populations in Canada.

have both suggested this policy change. The goal was that the change would help ensure the nation's infrastructure can support incoming residents.

Inequality for Indigenous peoples also remains a pressing issue for Canadian society. The government has taken steps to remedy some past harms. In 2006, the Indian Residential Schools Settlement Agreement included a roughly $2 billion compensation package for victims of Canada's residential school system.[13] The Truth and Reconciliation Commission raised awareness about what happened in residential schools and made recommendations to mend relations with Indigenous people.

In the past, the Canadian government failed to provide First Nations with money for child and family services. In 2022, the government announced that it would distribute billions of dollars to First Nations. Many problems still remain. Indigenous Canadians have higher rates of unemployment, poorer health outcomes, and inadequate housing. Violence against Indigenous women has been described as an epidemic by the United Nations. Additionally, pipelines and other economic activities threaten the land and water resources of Indigenous communities.

Despite these economic, environmental, and social challenges, Canada continues to rank among the top countries in the world to live. On the international stage, it is routinely recognized as having a positive influence on world affairs. During its history, Canada has developed a reputation for resolving conflicts and fighting inequality, tasks that it will continue to pursue in the years to come.

ESSENTIAL **FACTS**

OFFICIAL NAME: CANADA

GEOGRAPHY

Area: 3,855,103 square miles (9,984,670 sq km)

Highest Elevation: Mount Logan at 19,551 feet (5,959 m)

Lowest Elevation: Atlantic, Pacific, and Arctic Oceans at 0 feet (0 m)

PEOPLE

Population: 38,794,813 (2024 est.)

Most Populous City: Toronto (6.4 million)

Ethnic Groups: Canadian, English, Scottish, French, Irish, German, Chinese, Italian, First Nations, Indian, Ukrainian, Métis

Religions: Christianity, Islam, Hinduism, Sikhism, Buddhism, Judaism, Traditional (North American Indigenous), other, none

GOVERNMENT

Type of Government: Federal parliamentary democracy under a constitutional monarchy

Capital: Ottawa

Head of State: British monarch, represented by the governor general

Head of Government: Prime minister

Legislature: Bicameral Parliament consisting of a Senate and House of Commons

ECONOMY

Currency: Canadian dollar

Major Industries: Transportation equipment, chemicals, processed and unprocessed minerals, food products, wood and paper products, natural gas

Natural Resources: Metals, uranium, potash, diamonds, fish, timber, coal, petroleum, natural gas, hydropower

NATIONAL SYMBOLS

National Anthem: “O Canada”

National Tree: Maple tree

National Animal: Beaver

GLOSSARY

archipelago
A group of islands, or a stretch of sea containing many islands.

deferential
Expressing respect and high regard to a superior.

electoral
Related to an election.

fjord
A long, deep, and narrow sea inlet sitting between very high cliffs.

gross domestic product (GDP)
The monetary value of all final goods and services produced within a nation's geographic borders over a specified period of time.

hierarchical
Relating to the classification of a group according to professional or social standing.

Indigenous
Relating to the earliest people living in a place.

LGBTQ
An acronym referring to lesbian, gay, bisexual, transgender, and queer or questioning people.

monarch
A person who reigns over a kingdom, such as a king or a queen.

pension
A regular payment made to a retired person as a reward for past services, or to help someone suffering from an injury or other need.

reconciliation
The process of restoring harmony or repairing a relationship.

socialist
Supporting an economic system in which the government controls the economy.

sovereignty
The power of a state or group to govern itself.

vocational
Related to a skill or trade that can be pursued as a career.

ADDITIONAL **RESOURCES**

SELECTED BIBLIOGRAPHY

Bercuson, David J., et al. "Canada." *Britannica*, 17 Jan. 2025, britannica.com. Accessed 17 Jan. 2025.

DK Eyewitness Canada. Penguin Random House, 2022.

Slaymaker, Olav, et al. "Physiographic Regions." *Canadian Encyclopedia*, 27 Feb. 2012, thecanadianencyclopedia.ca. Accessed 17 Jan. 2025.

FURTHER READINGS

Buckey, A. W. *Land Preservation*. Abdo, 2025.

Sainsbury, Brendan, et al. *Lonely Planet Canada*. Lonely Planet, 2024.

Zweig, Eric. *Hockey Hall of Fame Heroes: Scorers, Goalies and Defensemen*. Firefly, 2021.

ONLINE RESOURCES

To learn more about Canada, please visit **abdobooklinks.com** or scan this QR code. These links are routinely monitored and updated to provide the most current information available.

MORE INFORMATION

For more information on this subject, contact or visit the following organizations:

Canadian Museum of History

100 Laurier St.
Gatineau, QC K1A 0M8
historymuseum.ca

The Canadian Museum of History is a national museum of anthropology, Canadian history, cultural studies, and ethnology in Gatineau, Quebec, Canada.

Hockey Hall of Fame

Brookfield Place
30 Yonge St.
Toronto, ON M5E 1X8
hhof.com/visit/visit.html

The Hockey Hall of Fame is the home of the Stanley Cup and a collection that tells the history of hockey in Canada and the formation of the National Hockey League (NHL).

House of Commons Building

111 Wellington St.
Ottawa, ON K1A 0A9
visit.parl.ca/sites/Visit/default/en_CA/HOC

The House of Commons at West Block is on Parliament Hill and is where Canadian MPs meet to discuss and vote on laws.

SOURCE **NOTES**

CHAPTER 1. A TOUR OF CANADA

1. David J. Bercuson et al. "Canada." *Britannica*, 17 Jan. 2025, britannica.com. Accessed 17 Jan. 2025.
2. Denyse Légaré. "The Basilica of Notre-Dame de Montréal." Translated by Rachel Tunnicliffe. *Quebec Religious Heritage Foundation*, n.d., web.archive.org. Accessed 17 Jan. 2025.
3. "Residential School Totem Pole." *Art Public Montréal*, 2016, artpublicmontreal.ca. Accessed 17 Jan. 2025.
4. "Montreal Tourism Back to Pre-Pandemic Numbers, Summer's Busiest Weekend Saw Record Numbers for Events." *CityNews Montreal*, 14 Aug. 2023, montreal.citynews.ca. Accessed 17 Jan. 2025.
5. Isa Tousignant. "Guide to the Underground City." *Tourisme Montréal*, 27 Aug. 2024, mtl.org. Accessed 17 Jan. 2025.
6. Adam Augustyn. "Montreal Canadiens." *Britannica*, 14 Jan. 2025, britannica.com. Accessed 17 Jan. 2025.
7. "Bell Centre." *Tourisme Montréal*, n.d., mtl.org. Accessed 17 Jan. 2025.
8. Jesslyn Shields. "What Are the 7 Largest Countries in the World by Area?" *HowStuffWorks*, n.d., science.howstuffworks.com. Accessed 17 Jan. 2025.

CHAPTER 2. GEOGRAPHY

1. "Canada." *CIA World Factbook*, 15 Jan. 2025, cia.gov. Accessed 17 Jan. 2025.
2. Peter Adams and Maxwell J. Dunbar. "Arctic Archipelago." *Canadian Encyclopedia*, 26 Oct. 2015, thecanadianencyclopedia.ca. Accessed 17 Jan. 2025.
3. "Canada-Denmark (Greenland)." *Sovereign Limits*, n.d., sovereignlimits.com. Accessed 17 Jan. 2025.
4. Olav Slaymaker et al. "Physiographic Regions." *Canadian Encyclopedia*, 29 Apr. 2024, thecanadianencyclopedia.ca. Accessed 17 Jan. 2025.
5. Andy Fyon. "Ice Age: Glacial Erratic." *Canada (Ontario) Beneath Our Feet*, 5 Nov. 2021, ontariobeneathourfeet.com. Accessed 17 Jan. 2025.
6. Slaymaker et al., "Physiographic Regions."
7. "Great Lakes—St. Lawrence." *Ducks Unlimited Canada*, n.d., ducks.ca. Accessed 17 Jan. 2025.
8. N. W. Rutter and Nathan Baker. "Glaciers in Canada." *Canadian Encyclopedia*, 1 Feb. 2018, thecanadianencyclopedia.ca. Accessed 17 Jan. 2025.
9. "Mount Logan." *Britannica*, 27 Sept. 2023, britannica.com. Accessed 17 Jan. 2025.
10. "Water: Frequently Asked Questions." *Government of Canada*, 13 Aug. 2018, canada.ca. Accessed 17 Jan. 2025.
11. John P. Rafferty. "World's Largest Lakes." *Britannica*, 28 July 2023, britannica.com. Accessed 17 Jan. 2025.
12. "Tourism Research." *Niagara Falls*, n.d., niagarafallstourism.com. Accessed 17 Jan. 2025.
13. "Water: Frequently Asked Questions."
14. Indira Duarte. "The Warmest Cities in Canada." *Canadim*, 13 Dec. 2023, canadim.com. Accessed 17 Jan. 2025.
15. David J. Bercuson et al. "Canada." *Britannica*, 17 Jan. 2025, britannica.com. Accessed 17 Jan. 2025.
16. Bercuson et al., "Canada."
17. "Canada-United States Relations." *Government of Canada*, 9 Sept. 2024, international.gc.ca. Accessed 17 Jan. 2025.
18. Liza Piper. "Great Slave Lake." *Canadian Encyclopedia*, 9 May 2016, thecanadianencyclopedia.ca. Accessed 17 Jan. 2025.

CHAPTER 3. PLANTS AND ANIMALS

1. David J. Bercuson et al. "Canada." *Britannica*, 17 Jan. 2025, britannica.com. Accessed 17 Jan. 2025.
2. "22 Reasons Why Conservation in Canada Matters to the Planet." *Wildlife Conservation Society Canada*, 22 May 2022, wcscanada.org. Accessed 17 Jan. 2025.
3. "Wild Species 2020: The General Status of Species in Canada." *Government of Canada*, 2 Dec. 2022, canada.ca. Accessed 17 Jan. 2025.
4. "Conservation in Canada Matters."
5. "Wildlife." *World Wildlife Fund Canada*, n.d., wwf.ca. Accessed 17 Jan. 2025.
6. "Canada." *Arctic Institute*, 1 Jan. 2024, thearcticinstitute.org. Accessed 13 Feb. 2024.
7. Annie Langlois. "Hinterland Who's Who: Arctic Tundra." *Canadian Wildlife Federation*, 2012, hww.ca. Accessed 17 Jan. 2025.
8. J. Terasmae and Andrew Reeves. "Tundra." *Canadian Encyclopedia*, 21 Dec. 2017, thecanadianencyclopedia.com. Accessed 17 Jan. 2025.
9. George H. La Roi. "Boreal Zone." *Canadian Encyclopedia*, 25 May 2018, thecanadianencyclopedia.ca. Accessed 17 Jan. 2025.
10. "Boreal Birds: North America's Bird Nursery." *Boreal Songbird Initiative*, n.d., borealbirds.org. Accessed 17 Jan. 2025.
11. "Boreal Birds."
12. *Featured Species-Associated Forest Habitats: Boreal Forest and Coastal Temperate Forest*. Alaska Department of Fish and Game, n.d., adfg.alaska.gov. Accessed 17 Jan. 2025.
13. "Coastal Temperate Rainforests." *Science World*, n.d., scienceworld.ca. Accessed 17 Jan. 2025.
14. "World Class Wildlife of Great Bear Rainforest." *Great Bear Tales*, 16 Sept. 2022, greatbeartales.com. Accessed 17 Jan. 2025.
15. Larry Kaumeyer. "What's Happening to Canada's Vanishing Wetlands?" *Ducks Unlimited Canada*, 26 Jan. 2022, ducks.ca. Accessed 17 Jan. 2025.
16. "Horned Puffin." *Cincinnati Zoo & Botanical Garden*, n.d., cincinnatizoo.org. Accessed 17 Jan. 2025.
17. Trevor Herriot. "Canada's Beautiful Prairie Grasslands Are among the Most Endangered Ecosystems in the World." *CBC*, n.d., cbc.ca. Accessed 17 Jan. 2025.

CHAPTER 4. HISTORY

1. David J. Bercuson et al. "Canada." *Encyclopedia Britannica*, 17 Jan. 2025, britannica.com. Accessed 17 Jan. 2025.
2. Robert McGhee. "History of Early Indigenous Peoples in Canada." *Canadian Encyclopedia*, 12 Dec. 2024, thecanadianencyclopedia.ca. Accessed 17 Jan. 2025.
3. Bercuson et al., "Canada."
4. "Discover Canada—Canada's History." *Government of Canada*, 26 Oct. 2015, canada.ca. Accessed 17 Jan. 2025.
5. "Canada's History."
6. "Canada's History."
7. Patricia E. Roy. "Internment in Canada." *Canadian Encyclopedia*, 4 Oct. 2024, thecanadianencyclopedia.ca. Accessed 17 Jan. 2025.
8. "Service Files of the Second World War—War Dead, 1939–1947." *Library and Archives Canada*, 18 Oct. 2022, bac-lac.gc.ca. Accessed 17 Jan. 2025.
9. "Military History Library: Bluebirds." *Valour Canada*, n.d., valourcanada.ca. Accessed 17 Jan. 2025.
10. Kenneth John Rea. "Nunavut." *Britannica*, 17 Jan. 2025, britannica.com. Accessed 17 Jan. 2025.

SOURCE **NOTES** CONTINUED

CHAPTER 5. PEOPLE AND CULTURE

1. "Infographic 1: 'Canadian' Tops the More Than 450 Ethnic or Cultural Origins Reported by the Population of Canada." *Statistics Canada*, 26 Oct. 2022, www150.statcan.gc.ca. Accessed 17 Jan. 2025.
2. "Ethnocultural and Religious Diversity—2021 Census Promotional Material." *Statistics Canada*, 14 Nov. 2022, statcan.gc.ca. Accessed 17 Jan. 2025.
3. "Canada." *CIA World Factbook*, 15 Jan. 2025, cia.gov. Accessed 17 Jan. 2025.
4. "While English and French Are Still the Main Languages Spoken in Canada, the Country's Linguistic Diversity Continues to Grow." *Government of Canada*, 17 Aug. 2022, www150.statcan.gc.ca. Accessed 17 Jan. 2025.
5. "Linguistic Diversity Continues to Grow."
6. "Linguistic Diversity Continues to Grow."
7. "First Nations." *Government of Canada*, 16 Jan. 2024, rcaanc-cirnac.gc.ca. Accessed 17 Jan. 2025.
8. "An Update on the Socio-Economic Gaps between Indigenous Peoples and the Non-Indigenous Population in Canada: Highlights from the 2021 Census." *Government of Canada*, 25 Oct. 2023, sac-isc.gc.ca. Accessed 17 Jan. 2025.
9. "Canada's Large Urban Centres Continue to Grow and Spread." *Statistics Canada*, 9 Feb. 2022, www150.statcan.gc.ca. Accessed 17 Jan. 2025.
10. *2021 Census: Citizenship, Immigration, Ethnic Origin, Visible Minority Groups (Race), Mobility, Migration, Religion*. City of Toronto, 4 Nov. 2022, toronto.ca. Accessed 17 Jan. 2025.
11. "National Men's Hockey Team." *Hockey Canada*, n.d., hockeycanada.ca. Accessed 17 Jan. 2025.
12. "National Women's Hockey Team." *Hockey Canada*, n.d., hockeycanada.ca. Accessed 17 Jan. 2025.
13. "Men's Field History." *World Lacrosse*, n.d., worldlacrosse.sport. Accessed 17 Jan. 2025.
14. "Women's Field History." *World Lacrosse*, n.d., worldlacrosse.sport. Accessed 17 Jan. 2025.

CHAPTER 6. POLITICS

1. "Contemporary Context: Commonwealth of Nations." *UK Parliament*, n.d., parliament.uk. Accessed 17 Jan. 2025.
2. "Member States of the Commonwealth." *Britannica*, 31 Oct. 2023, britannica.com. Accessed 17 Jan. 2025.
3. "Parliament: An Overview." *Parliament of Canada*, n.d., lop.parl.ca. Accessed 17 Jan. 2025.
4. J. E. Hodgetts. "Parliament of Canada." *Britannica*, 13 Jan. 2025, britannica.com. Accessed 17 Jan. 2025.
5. "Canadian Political Parties." *Canada Guide*, n.d., thecanadaguide.com. Accessed 17 Jan. 2025.
6. "The Canadian Military." *Canada Guide*, n.d., thecanadaguide.com. Accessed 17 Jan. 2025.
7. "Canadian Armed Forces 101." *Government of Canada*, 30 Sept. 2021, canada.ca. Accessed 17 Jan. 2025.
8. "How Many Fighter Jets Does Canada Have (2024)?" *Abbotsford International Airshow*, 15 May 2024, abbotsfordairshow.com. Accessed 17 Jan. 2025.

CHAPTER 7. ECONOMICS

1. "Canada GDP: Summary." *Trading Economics*, n.d., tradingeconomics.com. Accessed 17 Jan. 2025.
2. "The Economy of Canada." *Canada Guide*, n.d., thecanadaguide.com. Accessed 17 Jan. 2025.
3. "Tourism Activity, 2023." *Statistics Canada*, 27 Sept. 2024, www150.statcan.gc.ca. Accessed 17 Jan. 2025.
4. "Add/Remove Data: Labour Force Characteristics by Industry, Annual (x1,000)." *Statistics Canada*, 10 Jan. 2025, www150.statcan.gc.ca. Accessed 17 Jan. 2025.
5. "The Economy of Canada."
6. "Statistical Overview of the Canadian Maple Industry, 2023." *Government of Canada*, 14 June 2024, agriculture.canada.ca. Accessed 17 Jan. 2025.
7. David J. Bercuson et al. "Canada." *Britannica*, 17 Jan. 2025, britannica.com. Accessed 17 Jan. 2025.
8. Brian Frederick Windley. "Precambrian." *Britannica*, 3 Jan. 2025, britannica.com. Accessed 17 Jan. 2025.
9. Bercuson et al., "Canada."
10. "The Economy of Canada."
11. "Ontario and Michigan Partner for Auto Industry Growth and Innovation." *Former Governors of Michigan*, 3 Aug. 2016, michigan.gov. Accessed 17 Jan. 2025.
12. "2024 Investment of Climate Statements: Canada." *US Department of State*, n.d., state.gov. Accessed 17 Jan. 2025.
13. "The Economy of Canada."

CHAPTER 8. CANADA TODAY

1. Einar H. Dyvik. "20 Countries with the Highest Monthly Salaries of Employees Worldwide in 2023." *Statista*, 18 Nov. 2024, statista.com. Accessed 17 Jan. 2025.
2. "Safest Countries in the World 2024." *World Population Review*, 2024, worldpopulationreview.com. Accessed 17 Jan. 2025.
3. "Canada Labor Laws: Maternity Leave and Parental Leave." *Payroll Edge*, 6 June 2024, thepayrolledge.com. Accessed 17 Jan. 2025.
4. "Canada." *CIA World Factbook*, 15 Jan. 2025, cia.gov. Accessed 17 Jan. 2025.
5. "Canada Population 2024 (Live)." *World Population Review*, 2024, worldpopulationreview.com. Accessed 17 Jan. 2025.
6. "Elementary–Secondary Education Survey, 2020/2021." *Statistics Canada*, 13 Oct. 2022, www150.statcan.gc.ca. Accessed 17 Jan. 2025.
7. David J. Bercuson et al. "Canada." *Britannica*, 17 Jan. 2025, britannica.com. Accessed 17 Jan. 2025.
8. "Best Global Universities in Canada, Ranked." *US News*, n.d., usnews.com. Accessed 17 Jan. 2025.
9. "Which Countries Have the Highest (and Lowest) Literacy Rates in the World?" *US Career Institute*, Feb. 2024, uscareerinstitute.edu. Accessed 17 Jan. 2025.
10. "About." *West Edmonton Mall*, n.d., wem.ca. Accessed 17 Jan. 2025.
11. "Energy Fact Book, 2024–2025: Key Energy, Economic, and Environmental Indicators." *Government of Canada*, 8 Oct. 2024, energy-information.canada.ca. Accessed 17 Jan. 2025.
12. "Why Is Anti-Immigration Sentiment on the Rise in Canada?" *YouTube*, uploaded by The Guardian, 6 Aug. 2024, youtube.com. Accessed 17 Jan. 2025.
13. Ian Austen. "Canada Settles $2 Billion Suit over 'Cultural Genocide' at Residential Schools." *New York Times*, 21 Jan. 2023, nytimes.com. Accessed 17 Jan. 2025.

INDEX

ABOUT THE **AUTHOR**

KURT WALDENDORF

Kurt Waldendorf is the author of more than a dozen books for children. When he's not writing or editing, he enjoys indoor rock climbing and running along the shore of Lake Michigan with his dog. He lives in Chicago, Illinois.